5-Star Revi

Th

Carrie A. Picardi's book, Leadership Essentials You Always Wanted to Know. For professionals interested in a better understanding of types of leadership and ways to become a more effective leader in normal times and times of change, this is an excellent book. As leaders explore how they can become more effective in meeting the challenges of a crisis, which is occurring with our current pandemic, it is helpful to begin looking closer at ourselves as leaders.

Dr. Picardi is effective in her descriptions of the various leadership attributes and leadership styles. She covers the main styles which are taught at both the Bachelor's and Master's levels. The structure of the book is effective as she introduces what leadership is, the attributes of leaders, development of leadership behavior theory, power and influence, and covers situational and contingency as well as charismatic and transformational leadership very effectively. Once we learn about the basics, she leads us with action steps as we develop our teams for leadership, develop a highly ethical leadership style (essential for every organization) and finally lead a thriving organization. Each chapter ends with a summary of the important points and a quiz for those who want to test their ability.

Some theory books are written to simply follow the regular academic class; however, this book points the reader to take action as they consider who they are and how they can become a more effective leader. I can easily see Leadership Essentials You Always Wanted to Know by Dr. Carrie A. Picardi being used in corporate department meetings, retreats, noncredit classes, and seminars very effectively as it focuses on the important leadership models which can make us more effective leaders. A concise and well-explained book!

This review is for an earlier edition.

SELF-LEARNING MANAGEMENT SERIES

LEADERSHIP ESSENTIALS

YOU ALWAYS WANTED TO KNOW

DR. CARRIE A. PICARDI

VIBRANT
PUBLISHERS

Leadership
Essentials

You Always Wanted To Know

Paperback ISBN 10: 1-63651-031-0
Paperback ISBN 13: 978-1-63651-031-6

Ebook ISBN 10: 1-63651-032-9
Ebook ISBN 13: 978-1-63651-032-3

Hardback ISBN 10: 1-63651-033-7
Hardback ISBN 13: 978-1-63651-033-0

Library of Congress Control Number: 2021930379

Vibrant Publishers books are available at special quantity discount for sales promotions, or for use in corporate training programs. For more information please write to bulkorders@vibrantpublishers.com

Please email feedback / corrections (technical, grammatical or spelling) to spellerrors@vibrantpublishers.com

To access the complete catalogue of Vibrant Publishers, visit www.vibrantpublishers.com

SELF-LEARNING MANAGEMENT SERIES

TITLE	PAPERBACK* ISBN

ACCOUNTING, FINANCE & ECONOMICS

COST ACCOUNTING AND MANAGEMENT ESSENTIALS	9781636511030
FINANCIAL ACCOUNTING ESSENTIALS	9781636510972
FINANCIAL MANAGEMENT ESSENTIALS	9781636511009
MACROECONOMICS ESSENTIALS	9781636511818
MICROECONOMICS ESSENTIALS	9781636511153
PERSONAL FINANCE ESSENTIALS	9781636511849

ENTREPRENEURSHIP & STRATEGY

BUSINESS PLAN ESSENTIALS	9781636511214
BUSINESS STRATEGY ESSENTIALS	9781949395778
ENTREPRENEURSHIP ESSENTIALS	9781636511603

GENERAL MANAGEMENT

BUSINESS LAW ESSENTIALS	9781636511702
DECISION MAKING ESSENTIALS	9781636510026
LEADERSHIP ESSENTIALS	9781636510316
PRINCIPLES OF MANAGEMENT ESSENTIALS	9781636511542
TIME MANAGEMENT ESSENTIALS	9781636511665

*Also available in Hardback & Ebook formats

SELF-LEARNING MANAGEMENT SERIES

TITLE	PAPERBACK* ISBN

HUMAN RESOURCE MANAGEMENT

DIVERSITY IN THE WORKPLACE ESSENTIALS	9781636511122
HR ANALYTICS ESSENTIALS	9781636510347
HUMAN RESOURCE MANAGEMENT ESSENTIALS	9781949395839
ORGANIZATIONAL BEHAVIOR ESSENTIALS	9781636510378
ORGANIZATIONAL DEVELOPMENT ESSENTIALS	9781636511481

MARKETING & SALES MANAGEMENT

DIGITAL MARKETING ESSENTIALS	9781949395747
MARKETING MANAGEMENT ESSENTIALS	9781636511788
SALES MANAGEMENT ESSENTIALS	9781636510743
SERVICES MARKETING ESSENTIALS	9781636511733

OPERATIONS & PROJECT MANAGEMENT

AGILE ESSENTIALS	9781636510057
OPERATIONS & SUPPLY CHAIN MANAGEMENT ESSENTIALS	9781949395242
PROJECT MANAGEMENT ESSENTIALS	9781636510712
STAKEHOLDER ENGAGEMENT ESSENTIALS	9781636511511

*Also available in Hardback & Ebook formats

What experts say about this book!

The capacity of Leadership is the most important ingredient to organizational well-being and success. Leadership is a philosophy of use of power, a set of learnable, observable competencies, skills and behaviors. Anyone can develop themselves as a leader. You become a leader when people choose to follow you. There is no topic that has been written about as extensively. The newly authored, Leadership Essentials, offers the reader a wonderful smorgasbord of all things leadership. It is a perfect way to begin your leadership studies.

– Leslie Yerkes
President, Catalyst Consulting Group, Inc.

Dr. Picardi has produced a helpful handbook for those who aspire to leadership positions in their organizations. It is a careful blend of theory, practice, and examples. Leadership concepts are concisely presented and the book is easy to read. The chapters on situational and contingency leadership and leading a thriving organization by themselves make this book a worthwhile read.

– Dr. Mark Koscinski
Assistant Professor of Accounting Practice

Carrie captualates decades of experience in this interesting and compelling read. It's not just a text book, but a story. It pulls together the essence of the key research on this topic.

The key learning objectives and chapter summary makes internalizing the material an easy task.

– Reo Oravec
Author, Speaker and Adjunct Professor of Discussion Sciences

What experts say about this book!

While the world is combatting Covid-19 and, as a consequence, facing one of its worst health and financial crises, strong leadership is now required more than ever before at all levels and in all countries. Dr. Picardi's work has arrived during a perfect storm exposing learners and practitioners of leadership to the essential aspects of leadership. There is much confusion in both the academic literature and popular press as to what constitutes 'good and effective' leadership. Dr. Picardi's book takes the reader back to the basics and unpacks the many mysteries of this popular topic. This book covers the key concepts of leadership and makes a strong and timely contribution to a more comprehensive understanding of contemporary leadership.

> **– Prof. Dr. Franco Gandolfi**
> **Professor, Georgetown University**

A book that really does what it says on the tin. The Essentials of Leadership are truly covered as the author takes the reader on a journey through the recognised theoretical concepts and ideas in a way that makes them both interesting and relevant. It is good to see that the influence of power is not forgotten and that ethical leadership is considered at a time when many leaders are being faced with demonstrating their ability to create value for society as much as value for their shareholders. An essential title for any leader's bookshelf and one that adds true value to the associated discourse on Leadership Practice and its role in organisational success.

> **– Dr. Gary Ramsden**
> **Associate Professor, Logistics and Operations Management**
> **Lincoln International Business School**

What experts say about this book!

An exceptional work on the foundation and practice of leadership within today's society. The author does a wonderful job in moving skillfully from the overall purpose of leadership, to the attributes & behaviors of those who are effective at it, onto the various situations that can arise within this area of management, with emphasis on the attributes needed to successfully handle them. What's most impressive to me is that all of this is covered in a concise, readable 200-page format, making it a 'go-to' resource for any college professor teaching a course on this subject. I highly recommend this dynamic, user-friendly text and plan on using it myself in the future.

– Prof. Anthony Rondinelli
Department of Business Administration
Springfield Technical Community College

Dr. Picardi has created a remarkable text. She accomplishes the most difficult task of translating her mastery of the subject matter into a form suitable for undergraduate students (or anyone else, for that matter) interested understanding leadership. Her text is straightforward, accurate, and oriented toward a practical application of the material.

This book is designed for those who value their time and wish to gain an understanding of leadership principles that can be effectively put into practice. Well done!

– Wade M. Chumney, J.D., M.Sc.
Associate Professor of Business Ethics and Law
California State University, Northridge

What experts say about this book!

This is the best Leadership book I have ever read! It compiles all the practical Leadership information, ideas, and guides that anyone would ever need. It includes the advice you need to be an excellent Leader. There are charts, summaries, and quizzes to organize your thinking. All the Chapters you would expect in a Leadership book are there. It even has a reference to an old friend on mine, Ken Blanchard, The One Minute Manager, who is an expert in Leadership and Training!! This book is a highly practical book on Leadership which I want to expose to all my own students. It is germane to any industry.

> – **Frank E. Cuzzi**
> **Professor of Marketing and Sports Management**
> **Monroe College and Berkeley College**

A well-rounded book on leadership, Dr. Picardi has done an excellent job of introducing the complexities of leadership, walking readers through various characteristics of leadership, and culminating in leadership development, ethical leadership, and leading a thriving organization. Written in a style that is welcoming and easy to follow along, Dr. Picardi's presentation of concepts models for students how to support concepts by referencing seminal works throughout the text. I highly recommend Leadership Essentials for use as undergraduate or graduate level introductory classes on leadership!

> – **Dr. Joseph H. Schuessler**
> **Associate Dean College of Business**
> **Tarleton State University**

What experts say about this book!

Dr. Picardi creates a monolithic learning path that enhances the student's potential for success by building a model that is inclusive in all facets of both the leader and leadership within it's role. Her focus on building the mindset, character and traits of a leader as foundations of a leader's styles and role of impact; creates a platform for the student's journey of understanding how a leader influences teams and an organization's performance. Her sequitur of the leader and leadership model is comprehensive to the point of filling the lacuna of leadership pedagogy and learning. As a recognized leader in business and entrepreneurship higher education, I recommend this book to anyone teaching a leadership course. It is one of the few leadership books I have read that has such a impactful journey of discovery and learning for the benefit of the student.

– Bob Milner
CEO TerBo Enterprises & MRH Automotive

This book is an important source of information on a topic which is ever more important in today's rapidly changing world where leadership is not an option for organizations to be able to navigate successfully and remain competitive.

This book represents an important guide for anyone who wishes to understand what are the key principles of leadership and to also better understand how they can improve their own leadership skills.

– Dr David Forgaty
Enterprise Marketing Analytics Leader
Evernorth Corporation

What experts say about this book!

Reading the title for the first time, I thought, "What are the Leadership Essentials?" As if reading the readers' mind, Dr. Picardi uses the first 87 pages to explain her list. By the time I was done reading what they meant, I was drawn to read more of the text. Where can I find the best leader or a list of leadership essentials?

One of the aspects defining Leadership essentials is the list in sections 1-10 of the text. It describes the essential for the 21st Century. The author shares relevant literature on these essentials of: innovation, vision, inner variables, inspiration, and communication. All along this thought-provoking book, Dr. Picardi pulls together of some well-known management experts and CEOs and integrates their sayings and thoughts together to emphasize the importance of leadership, and leadership essentials.

Once she is done with the support and understanding of Leadership Essentials, the author delves into leading the "Thriving Organization." Here, she explains why transformational leaders are so important in today's work environments in contrast to transactional roles.

The book brings together some well-said business decision making dos and don'ts from the "already-been-there-done-that" management/ leader experts and founders. Overall, this is a well-researched book, and an essential read for the managers, leaders, executives, and entrepreneurs who wish to see the success in their decisions. Or, it is just for the rest of us who want to be more successful some day!

– **Robert Batiste, PhD**
Assistant Professor, Embry Riddle Aeronautical University
Capella University

About the Author

Dr. Carrie A. Picardi, Ph.D., is an industrial/ organizational psychologist with over 20 years of professional experience in human resource management, as a research analyst and consultant, and in academia as a tenured professor of management. She has led initiatives in the areas of leadership development, assessment center design and deployment, job analysis, talent acquisition and retention, compensation and total rewards, learning and development, performance management, and employee engagement. Her research focuses on employee performance management, and she has published several peer-reviewed research papers in this area as well as presented her findings at national conferences. In addition to Leadership Essentials, Dr. Picardi is the author of two textbooks, Research Methods: Designing and Conducting Research With a Real-World Focus (Sage, 2013) and Recruitment and Selection: Strategies for Workforce Planning and Assessment (Sage, 2019).

This page is intentionally left blank

Acknowledgement

I wish to express my sincere and heartfelt gratitude to my family for their love, support, and encouragement: my dear fiancé and better half, Richard Sutcliffe; my parents, Sam and Johanna Picardi; and my brother, sister-in-law, and nephew, Michael, Alison, and Liam Picardi. My special little rescue pups, Jada, Chloe, and Sammy, who never left my side as I typed away for hours on end and always kept me company with their loyalty and unconditional love.

This page is intentionally left blank

Table of Contents

This page is intentionally left blank

Chapter 1

The Meaning and Purpose of Leadership

Leadership has been the focus of interest and inquiry throughout history, dating as far back as ancient civilizations, in any time period and setting in which an individual possessed the capability to influence a number of followers for a distinct purpose. Even though that notion sounds straightforward and simple, several facets of leadership continue to be a mystery and a challenge for many to fully grasp and master. Why do you think that is? Part of the reason is due to the fact that leadership is a complex subject, with many interconnected elements and factors that influence the scope and effectiveness of a leader. In order to be a leader, one must have followers – so leadership does not involve just one individual.

In Chapter 1, we begin our exploration by defining leadership and reviewing fundamental principles and concepts that encompass what it means to lead, leadership roles, the circumstances where leaders exist, and the leader-follower relationship.

After reading this chapter, key learning objectives attained will include:

- Understanding the concept of leadership, including different ways in which leadership is defined.

- Comparing and differentiating between the roles of leader and manager.

- Understanding the many different roles of a leader.

- Examining the different settings and contexts in which leaders have made important contributions and impact throughout history.

- Comparing the similarities and differences of formal and informal leaders.

- Defining the role of the follower and examining the interactive relationship between a leader and their followers.

1.1 Leadership Defined

Before we embark on our exploration of leadership theories, concepts, models, and applications in real-world situations, it is important to consider the varying definitions of leadership that exist. Leadership has many dimensions, which makes this subject multi-layered and complex. There is no one-size-fits-all answer to effective leadership. Leaders are critically important in every area of society and their role and purpose may vary substantially as a result, depending on the setting and its context, the goals and objectives to be achieved, and many other factors that we will examine throughout this book.

As you begin to think about what it means to lead and all the unique elements that may comprise leadership, consider the following definitions and ideas:

- Leadership encompasses the ability to inspire confidence among their followers so that they may support the leader's vision and mission.

- A leader has the capability to influence others to understand and support a collective, shared purpose, and assist with the tasks and activities needed to be performed.

- A leader effectively facilitates the efforts of their followers through a combination of social and interpersonal skills, expertise in a specific area or field, and dedication to a particular mission and purpose, to accomplish shared objectives.

- Leadership involves developing a strategy, planning goals and desired outcomes, and giving meaningful direction to one or more individuals so that they may perform the needed tasks and duties designed to support achieving these goals and outcomes.

As you can see, there are many valuable ways to describe leadership, but they are all complementary and it is clear that common themes exist among these ideas. Moreover, these definitions are fairly broad and may easily apply to leaders in an array of different contexts and roles.

Leadership and management guru Peter Drucker stated that regardless of setting and context, all of the most effective leaders he had ever encountered held four basic attributes:

1. A leader must be someone with followers.

2. An effective leader is not known solely as being loved and admired by their followers, but also as someone who produces results and whose followers do the right things to help produce those results. They are doers.

3. Leaders are highly visible and set examples for their followers.

4. Leadership is not defined solely on money, rank, title, or privilege; leadership is a responsibility.

(The Peter F. Drucker Foundation, 1996).

Regardless of the type of leader, their role in society, and their mission, all of these definitions and ideas are still relevant and can be expanded upon with more specific detail for a greater deep-dive distinction based on the nature of the leader (e.g., military general, government leader, business manager, scientific pioneer, religious figure, sports icon). In the following sections, we will examine the diversity of roles that a leader may embody, and the different situations and environments where we can see the importance of having strong leadership.

1.2 Leadership Roles

One of the aspects of leadership that makes it a complex subject is its role diversity. There are myriad roles that a leader may hold at any given time, which requires they wear many different hats depending on the tasks and objectives they need to complete and their audience in a particular situation or circumstance.

One of the pioneers in leadership and managerial theory, Henry Mintzberg, developed the following list of leader roles:

• Figurehead	• Innovator
• Director	• Change Agent
• Spokesperson-Communicator	• Negotiator
• Liaison	• Resource Allocator
• Coach	• Problem Solver
• Team Builder/Team Player	• Entrepreneur
• Visionary	• Strategic Planner

(Mintzberg, 1973; Dubrin, 2007)

Many leaders assume two or more roles, often simultaneously, which requires a great deal of flexibility and the ability to pivot from one role to another seamlessly without compromising any other role's presence. In other words, just because one role is 'onstage' should not diminish the importance or presence of other roles that may be 'backstage' at any given time. Consider the role of a college professor, a tangible example of a leader with multiple roles. In the class environment, the principal roles may be communicator, organizer, and director. Outside of the classroom, a professor may also serve as coach, negotiator, and problem solver. If a professor is also a club adviser, for example, they may have the role of strategic planner, visionary, and team builder. That said, when the professor returns to the classroom, those key roles must return to focus and be adhered to accordingly by the students.

Depending on the situation's need and goals, a leader must be able to step into one or more of these roles as relevant and appropriate and facilitate support and actionable behaviors from followers. In the next section, we will examine an array of situations where leadership occurs and how leaders can be remarkably impactful in many different ways, even when they are leading in a unique context with a very specific purpose and focus.

1.3 Leadership Setting and Context

Leaders can be found in all areas of life and society, past and present. Some leaders have a direct, niched, and somewhat formal followership such as business/organizational leaders, religious leaders, and military leaders. Other leaders may influence in a broader and more indirect capacity, and have different types of followers, such as celebrities, sports figures, and trailblazers in a specific field (e.g., science, technology, education).

Table 1.1 highlights examples of the diversity of environments and context in which leaders have demonstrated impact and achievement throughout history:

Table 1.1

Business & Organizational Leaders	Religious & Spiritual Leaders	Civil Rights & Societal Leaders	Government & Military Leaders	Science Leaders, Inventors, & Pioneers	Sports & Entertainment Leaders
Henry Ford	Saint (Mother) Teresa of Calcutta	Harriet Tubman	Abraham Lincoln	Thomas Edison	Jackie Robinson
John D. Rockefeller	Mohandas Gandhi	Susan B. Anthony	Franklin Delano Roosevelt	Albert Einstein	Michael Jordan
Steve Jobs	Pope Francis	Dr. Martin Luther King, Jr.	John F. Kennedy	Amelia Earhart	Billie Jean King
Warren Buffett	The Dalai Lama	Rosa Parks	Margaret Thatcher	Marie Curie	Venus & Serena Williams
Elon Musk		Thurgood Marshall	Ronald Reagan	Nikola Tesla	Elvis Presley
Jack Welch		Nelson Mandela	Joan of Arc	Jonas Salk	Oprah Winfrey
Sheryl Sandberg			Napoleon Bonaparte	Neil deGrasse Tyson	Dwayne Johnson
Andrea Jung			General Colin Powell		Beyoncé & Jay-Z

As you can see from this diverse list, leaders emerge in all areas of society to fulfill a unique and valuable purpose. While their vision and path may be specific and focused on a very niche area of society, the outcomes they provide may reach and benefit a much broader population, in the present and for years to come. Additionally, these leader examples demonstrate that individuals can lead via a formal position or role assignment, and they can also emerge as leaders through informal and unstructured means. We will examine the nature of formal and informal leaders in the next section.

1.4 Formal and Informal Leaders

Can a person be a great leader without holding a formal title, rank, or assigned position? This is a common leadership question, and the answer is yes – an individual can be an effective leader with or without an official 'leader' title or designation. The leaders highlighted in the previous section provide clear validation of the impact of both effective formal and informal leaders throughout history. There are some key differences between a formal and an informal leader, most notably in the structure and system in which they are working, and the type and level of accountability they have to their followers or stakeholders.

First, a formal leader will have an official position, title, or rank that was designated or assigned to them in some structured manner such as by election (president, prime minister, mayor), job offer (manager, director), award (pioneer, inventor), or hierarchy (royalty). An informal leader may not hold an official position or title, and may not be leading in the context of a formal structure such as an organization or government office. Next, a formal leader will have responsibility for meeting or exceeding specific performance expectations from their various stakeholder groups (e.g., shareholders, employees, customers, government/regulatory agencies, the public/community, special interest groups) and are held accountable for targeted outcomes and goal attainment. Some of their needs will overlap, but typically each of these stakeholder groups will have a different set of expectations for the leader, and their key performance indicators (KPI's) will be based on corresponding goals and behaviors. For example, shareholders of a company such as Apple will expect their leaders to produce a positive return on investment as indicated by sales growth, profitability, and the launch of innovative new products outpacing any competitors. Customers may have a similar expectation to the shareholders in terms of new and innovative products coming to market regularly that meet their needs, but the rest of their expectations may be around quality, safety, excellent customer service, a positive and/or entertaining experience, good value for their money, having a sound reputation and brand image, and being a socially responsible company. An informal leader will also have a degree of responsibility for goal achievement and performance outcomes, but their level of accountability is driven more by their own internal motivation and less by potential actions of their stakeholder groups (e.g., customers may stop buying their products, investors may sell their stock).

While formal and informal leaders differ in the nature and scope of position and the structure of the environment/setting in which they lead, where they are similar is in what they do. Both formal and informal leaders may be responsible for creating a vision, planning and strategy which involves identifying a purpose and direction, determining the short and long-term goals and objectives necessary to fulfill that purpose, designing roles and organizing work/activities to accomplish these goals and objectives, and evaluating performance and outcomes regularly. Additionally, formal and informal leaders will also be responsible for addressing unplanned needs and situations in an ad hoc manner as changes arise that the leader must respond to swiftly and handle appropriately. An informal leader can be just as effective as a formal leader, without having a position of authority or level of status. In fact, informal leaders often naturally emerge from within a group in such an inspirational and impressionable way that those around them wholeheartedly become their followers because they want to, not because they have to do so. In the next section, we will examine the nature of a leader's followers.

1.5 The Leader-Follower Partnership

Leadership requires two elements: the leader and their followers. One component cannot exist without the other in place. While the nature of a leader's followers may vary depending on the type of leader, the environment, and the shared vision and purpose, there are core elements common to a wide array of followers regardless of context:

- Trust in the leader, that their decisions and actions will align with the group's vision and shared values and purpose, positively supporting their followers.

- Loyalty and commitment, grounded in a belief that one is part of a vision and mission bigger than themselves in which they can invest and fully support.

- Willingness to perform to a specified level of expectation, to uphold one's own work ethic to contribute meaningfully, and to shift one's behaviors as necessary in support of the collective focus and goals.

The relationship between a leader and their followers is an interactive exchange, as together they share the responsibility for managing ongoing objectives and needs in which there is mutual interest, dedication, and focus, and that also continue to unfold and evolve over time. As the leader and followers work collaboratively, they move closer towards achievement of shared goals, and attaining/sustaining their vision, mission, and purpose. To that end, an effective leader understands the importance of developing and maintaining a true and dynamic partnership with their followers. A partnership enables the leader to move away from pure authoritative mode and closer to shared input/ contribution, influence, and decision making. This does not just happen organically. It must be designed purposefully, and built with some sense of structure and expectations in place. Otherwise, those involved will not fully understand appropriate behaviors and boundaries.

The following elements should be established and sustained by a leader for a productive and harmonious partnership with their followers:

1. Communicating a clear and well-defined vision, mission, purpose, and set of values, ensuring support and shared belief (i.e., what we are doing and why it matters).

2. Creating a safe space that is non-threatening and non-retaliatory, enabling anyone to comfortably voice their perspectives, opinions, and ideas even if they are opposite of the leader or other followers.

3. Cultivating a climate of individual accountability, that empowers every member or follower to hold some level of responsibility for their own tasks, performance, and outcomes based on their role and extent of influence within the group, as well as some degree of collective accountability for shared goals and objectives.

4. Demonstrating honesty, transparency, and respect for everyone through decisions and actions, and encouraging the same behaviors among followers towards the leader as well as towards each other.

(Dubrin, 2007)

The most effective and respected leaders understand that the needs and challenges we face today in all areas of life and modern society are complex, often challenging, and constantly changing. They know that maintaining a genuine and supportive partnership with their followers is critically important to their purpose and making a difference. They will take care of their followers, provide the resources they need to succeed in their roles, empower them to make prudent decisions, and foster a sense of community. In turn, the followers will be engaged and focused on doing what needs to be done and adapt whenever the need for change arises.

We will consider the concept of effectiveness throughout this book, which essentially refers to the ability to attain desired results. In addition, a strong and impactful leader will also successfully balance effectiveness with efficiency and ethics. Efficiency, which is the prudent and logical use of resources (e.g., time, money, people/effort, materials) and ethics, which is working with integrity and adhering to sound morals and judgment, are just as important as effectiveness. Just because a leader is effective in their ability to demonstrate performance outcomes and goal achievement, does not automatically mean they are acting efficiently or ethically. These 'Three E's' - as depicted in Figure 1.1 - must all be in balance. A leader who demonstrates effectiveness and efficiency to meet sales quotas, production numbers, or deadlines by sacrificing quality control, policies, and safety procedures, or other critical protocol may be achieving a performance outcome at the expense of quality, safety, and/or appropriate treatment of their workforce and other constituents. Therefore, they are not really acting effectively because they are sacrificing ethical decisions and actions. Leadership is truly a complex subject with many components, and the role of leader in any capacity requires a multifaceted and agile individual capable of inspiring followers through many different circumstances. Whether a leader has two followers or two million, it is a big role with much responsibility!

Figure 1.1

As we review the many important leadership theories, concepts, and pivotal findings from researchers and the unique and valuable contributions of the leaders themselves throughout this book, the following core principles (Northouse, 2016) will continue to be emphasized:

1. Leadership involves an ongoing process, not a solitary event or circumstance.

2. Leadership requires some degree of influence and persuasion.

3. Leadership may occur in groups ranging in size from a few individual followers to an entire population.

4. Leadership requires focus and support from followers for shared goals and a plan for how to attain them.

While these overarching leadership principles conclude this chapter, we have now opened the door to explore essential leadership knowledge, competencies, and real-world applications that are relevant and valuable, today and in the future.

Chapter Summary

◆ Leadership is a complex subject with many interconnected elements and factors that influence the scope and effectiveness of a leader.

◆ Leaders are important in every area of society and their role and purpose may vary depending on the environs and its context, the goals and objectives to be achieved, and influencing factors within and outside the group or organization.

◆ There are a variety of unique roles that a leader may hold, requiring they wear many different hats depending on the tasks and objectives they need to complete and their audience in a particular situation or circumstance.

◆ Leaders can be found in all areas of life and society, past and present. Some leaders have direct and formal followers such as business leaders, religious leaders, and military leaders. Other leaders may influence in a broader and more indirect manner with a diverse follower group, such as celebrities, sports figures, and trailblazers in a specific field.

◆ A leader can be a formal designation through position or title, as well as informal through their natural emergence from a group and ability to inspire and influence.

◆ Leadership requires both a leader and followers, and an effective leader understands the importance of developing and maintaining a partnership with their followers to work collaboratively, productively, and harmoniously.

Quiz 1

1. A defining aspect of leadership is the ability to:

   a. communicate in multiple languages

   b. give orders to followers

   c. maintain status quo in an organization

   d. inspire people's confidence and gain their support

2. Which stakeholder group would be most likely focused on a leader's effectiveness in fostering and sustaining a positive, trusting, collaborative, and engaging culture within an organization?

   a. Government

   b. Shareholders

   c. Employees

   d. Customers

3. A leader who is an exceptionally strong and clear speaker, delivering compelling speeches, press conferences, interviews, and presentations, would thrive in the role of:

   a. Figurehead

   b. Entrepreneur

   c. Spokesperson

   d. Strategic Planner

4. **The ability to attain desired results is referred to as:**

   a. Ethics

   b. Efficiency

   c. Entrepreneurship

   d. Effectiveness

5. **Which of the following is an example of an informal leader?**

   a. A state governor

   b. A volunteer organizing a community event

   c. A college professor

   d. A shift supervisor for a fast food chain

Solutions to the above questions can be downloaded from
the **Online Resources** *section of this book on*
www.vibrantpublishers.com

This page is intentionally left blank

Chapter 2

Leader Attributes: Traits, Knowledge, Skills, and Abilities

Being an effective leader requires various personal traits and characteristics, areas of knowledge and expertise, skills, and abilities. The reason a multifaceted individual is so important for impactful leadership is because that person will need to respond, through carefully thought-out behaviors and actions, to many diverse situations and needs to influence different types of people as their followers to support their vision and purpose. A combination of certain traits, personal characteristics, abilities and skills may be needed to garner support from a group and achieve targeted goals in one particular setting, while another scenario may require a somewhat different combination. Even though all leaders possess a universal set of attributes, they also need to have adequate breadth and diversity of attributes to swiftly and competently pivot from one situation to another with agility and the appropriate response. This ability to wear many hats and shift into changing circumstances effectively will result in greater follower confidence in the leader and their investment or effort towards the leader's mission and goals.

In this chapter, we will examine foundational leadership traits and behavioral theories and models as well as key research findings that continue to be applied in innovative and progressive ways within organizations today. We will also gain a comprehensive understanding of the personality traits, skills, competencies, and abilities that are critically important for a leader to be successful in different types of organizations addressing diverse needs and achieving necessary goals and objectives.

After reading this chapter, key learning objectives attained will include:

- Understanding the findings from trait research and the specific traits shown to impact leader effectiveness.

- Describing the different personality trait models and how they can be used to understand the multifaceted trait needs of a positive and impactful leader.

- Categorizing the traits considered to be universally positive and universally negative in a global context.

- Understanding how a leader's knowledge, skills, and abilities should be in alignment with their traits to serve effectively and produce positive results.

- Describing how trait and skill-based models can be leveraged for conducting needs assessments and identifying areas of focus for strategic leadership training, development, and coaching.

2.1 Early Leadership Trait Research

Pioneering researchers (Stogdill, 1948; Kahn, 1956; Bass, 1990) have examined various factors that impact a leader's competence and effectiveness for decades, yielding important findings that are still being applied today in different contexts and circumstances. Trait studies emerged in early leadership research that provided valuable insights regarding the impact and importance of specific traits and characteristics on effective leader performance and outcomes.

So, what exactly is a trait? A trait is an individual characteristic or attribute that a person may exhibit through their behaviors in different situations and contexts. We all possess a collection of many different traits, and combined they comprise our unique self, which is how others see us.

One of the most widely respected researchers in this domain, Ralph Stogdill, conducted two pivotal survey research studies on leadership traits: an analysis of over 124 trait studies in 1948 and a follow-up analysis of 163 trait studies in 1974. From the 1948 study, Stogdill concluded that leaders differentiate themselves from followers on eight core traits:

• Intelligence	• Insight	• Initiative
• Self-confidence	• Alertness	• Responsibility
• Persistence	• Sociability	

In 1974, Stogdill compared follow-up findings with the original 1948 study findings and further refined the list to ten traits:

• Achievement	• Initiative	• Cooperativeness
• Sociability	• Persistence	• Self-confidence
• Tolerance	• Insight	• Responsibility
• Influence		

As you can see, individual traits represent a wide range of personal characteristics and attributes. Personality-specific traits comprise a significant part of the entire collection of traits and attributes that make up our whole self. Next, we will conduct a deep-dive exploration into personality traits as we consider how diverse personality traits are and how they integrate into a comprehensive picture of leadership attributes.

2.2 Unpacking Personality Traits

Personality traits are typically consistent in an individual and do not constantly shift around. For example, an individual who is emotionally stable will generally demonstrate calm behaviors across an array of scenarios; they won't get unraveled too easily. That said, personality traits are not 'set in stone'. Just because a person demonstrates a particular personality trait most of the time does not mean that they can never act out of character and show a deviation from that trait in a unique situation. If we consider the example of a person who is calm and stable the majority of the time, what might happen if they experienced a traumatic or shocking event, such as a car accident? That is an extremely intense and frightening situation that would likely result in panic and fear for anyone, even a person of strong emotional stability. This is an important point as we explore the personality traits of effective leaders. While we may be able to rely on a leader for a generally reliable and consistent set of personality traits, there may be egregious circumstances that require the temporary shifting of a trait to accommodate the situation.

One of the most widely recognized, respected, and leveraged personality trait models is the five-factor personality model, often referred to as the 'Big Five' personality model. Researchers (Allport & Odbert, 1933; Cattell, 1947; Fiske, 1949; Costa & McCrae, 1988; Barrick & Mount, 1991; Hogan, 1991) have been studying and categorizing personality traits for decades. They examined the extent to which personality research findings can be applied to different environments and contexts to better understand and predict individual motives, attitudes, tendencies, and behaviors. The Big Five personality trait model consists of five different personality dimensions, as depicted in Table 2.1. Each dimension can be examined along a low-moderate-high spectrum.

Figure 2.1

While there is an extraordinarily large number of terms and descriptive words to describe the different personality traits that exist, the Big Five is a well-known and validated model that has been used as the foundation for many questionnaires, inventories, and assessments, with valuable applications for personal self-awareness, professional development, and understanding organizational behavior and interpersonal dynamics.

Most of the time, our behaviors will land in approximately the same place on this continuum for any given dimension, but situational factors may influence us to shift our behaviors differently (Picardi, 2019). For example, a person may have a reserved, introverted personality most of the time, but around their family they demonstrate more extraverted behaviors and are talkative and gregarious. In that way, there is a sort of contextual flow built into the Big Five model.

Table 2.1

The Big Five Personality Model	
Agreeableness	The extent to which an individual is cooperative, flexible, and accommodating.
Conscientiousness	The extent to which an individual is dependable, demonstrates integrity and a strong work ethic, is organized, responsible, and achievement-oriented.
Emotional Stability	The extent to which an individual is calm, stable, grounded, and cool under pressure and intense situations.
Extraversion	The extent to which an individual is comfortable in verbally articulating their thoughts, is talkative, outgoing, and sociable.
Openness to Experience	The extent to which an individual is open-minded, an out-of-the-box thinker, creative, nonconforming to structure and routine, and willing to take risks.

(Barrick & Mount, 1991)

Another key contribution in the field of personality research has been the emergence of emotional intelligence. Daniel Goleman, researcher and best-selling author, pioneered the concept of emotional intelligence which provides an in-depth assessment of personality traits critically important to managing oneself and one's emotions in the context of their surroundings and among other people. According to Goleman (1995), emotional intelligence is comprised of four main traits with corresponding abilities, as described in Table 2.2:

Table 2.2

Emotional Intelligence	
Self-awareness	The ability to understand your strengths, limitations, emotional triggers, moods, behavioral tendencies, and how you come across to others.
Self-management	The ability to regulate your emotions, to diffuse stressful/negative situations to avoid emotional outbursts, and to be stable and adaptable.
Social awareness	The ability to have empathy for others, demonstrating that you can view a situation from the lens/perspective of others even when it is different; the ability to accurately assess the tone/climate of an individual or group to understand their needs, challenges, motivation.
Relationship management	The ability to have clear, honest, tactful, and genuine communication with others; possessing the interpersonal skills needed for rapport building, respect for others' input and feedback, conflict resolution, demonstrating compassion, and consideration towards others.

Research findings and applications in the area of emotional intelligence demonstrate its importance and value for not only leaders, but for everyone both personally and professionally. Because leaders also have the responsibility of sustaining a positive and productive relationship with their followers, emotional intelligence is especially important as they encourage the accomplishment of collective goals and support for a shared mission. If a leader does not have at least a moderate level of emotional intelligence, any relationship with their followers will be significantly compromised along with their vision and purpose.

In addition to these foundational personality trait models, other influential researchers (Sternberg, 2003; Dubrin, 2007) in the areas of trait theory and leadership have also identified an array of complementary traits for effective leadership that are worth noting:

• Accountability	• Creativity	• Insightful
• Assertive	• Credibility	• Inspirational
• Authenticity (being 'real')	• Decisiveness	• Patient
• Collaborative	• Diplomacy	• Resiliency
• Compassionate	• Enthusiasm	• Supportive
• Competence	• Flexibility	• Trustworthiness
• Confidence	• Humility	
• Courageous	• Inquisitive	

While many of these traits would likely be perceived as appealing and valued to a number of individuals and groups, some of these traits may be more or less relevant in certain environments or even perceived as more or less important to different groups, especially in the context of global geographic and cultural diversity. In the next section, we will explore fascinating global research findings on leadership traits.

2.3 Universal Leadership Traits

There are specific traits and attributes valued and respected in all leaders, regardless of geographic location, type of organization, context, or situation. The GLOBE (Global Leadership and Organizational Behavior Effectiveness) Project is a research think tank that conducts studies and publishes their findings on leadership and organizational effectiveness. We will examine a bit more research from the GLOBE Project in a later chapter of this book. GLOBE researchers have shared a valuable list of the leader attributes that are perceived as desired and valued among thousands of managers and leaders in 62 countries. In addition, their list, as shown below includes the characteristics and qualities universally perceived as negative and undesirable in leaders worldwide.

Universally Positive Leader Attributes	
• Trustworthy	• Dependable
• Just	• Intelligent
• Honest	• Decisive
• Foresighted	• Effective Bargainer
• Plans Ahead	• Win-Win Problem Solver
• Encouraging	• Administratively Skilled
• Positive	• Communicative
• Dynamic	• Informed
• Motive Arouser	• Coordinator
• Confidence Builder	• Team Builder
• Motivational	• Excellence-oriented

(House, et al., 2004)

Universally Negative Leader Attributes	
• Loner	• Non-explicit
• Asocial	• Egocentric
• Non-cooperative	• Ruthless
• Irritable	• Dictatorial

(House, et al., 2004)

All of these trait research findings and insights have contributed immensely to understanding the contributing factors of productive and impactful leadership. These findings also clearly demonstrate the importance of alignment and balance of traits and contextual factors as determinants of leadership. While many of these traits and personal characteristics are not typically areas that an individual can change in themselves through training and education, sometimes a person can 'reprogram' themselves to adjust any trait-based tendencies that do not serve them well, such as panicking under pressure or being impatient with others. In addition, individuals can definitely acquire new knowledge and hone their skills and abilities through developmental activities and coaching. Effective leadership behaviors can be successfully developed through the acquisition and mastery of relevant knowledge, skills, and abilities, which we will examine in the next section.

2.4 Knowledge, Skills, and Abilities of Effective Leaders

While trait models are very important to understanding leadership, they do not tell the whole story. Who we are as humans and our contribution to society is a much more complex picture, and should also encompass several other key elements: our knowledge, skills, and abilities, also referred to as KSA's. Early research by Katz (1955) in the Harvard Business Review examined leadership skills and produced pivotal findings that showed skills, unlike traits, could be wholly developed through training and education. The three categories of skills derived from this research included (1) technical skills, (2) human skills, and (3) conceptual skills. A detailed description of each skill area can be found below. Katz also emphasized that these skills were not substitutes for traits but rather complementary, and both are important components of effective leadership. This early research set the groundwork for increased attention to the KSA's aspect of leadership, and that leadership could be developed through proper education, skill-building, and coaching.

1. **Technical Skills**

   - Having relevant breadth and depth of knowledge, as well as the ability to perform tasks and functions, in the areas of:
     - Operations
     - Processes, workflow, and methods
     - Equipment
     - Technology tools and systems
     - Methods and techniques for performing tasks

2. **Human Skills**

   - Developing and fostering positive interpersonal relationships

   - Communicating clearly with focus and purpose

   - Acting as a coach and adviser to followers, investing in their development and growth

- Demonstrating objectivity and fairness to resolve conflicts and challenges

- Inspiring followers to contribute towards shared goals by serving as a motivational influence

- Enabling followers to wholeheartedly share ideas and provide input without judgement

3. Conceptual Skills

- Developing a vision that depicts a tangible an appealing improvement to a situation or need

- Having insight to forecast trends and patterns and anticipate changes

- Seeing opportunities and generating ideas for how to make them a reality

- Planning a strategy and both short and long-term goals

- Possessing critical and analytical thinking, logic and reasoning

- Making informed and timely decisions even without sufficient information/facts or resources

From this early work, these key categories have been adopted as sound and relevant areas of KSA focus for all types of leaders in different scenarios and contexts. In an organization, these categories are also well-suited to leaders and managers at different levels, including team leaders, first-line, and middle managers. These findings created opportunities for many other researchers to further examine the implications of appropriate knowledge, skills, and abilities for effective leadership.

More recently, a relevant and valuable skill-building tool for use in leadership development to emerge is the Skill-based Leadership Model, developed by researchers Mumford, Zaccaro, Harding, Jacobs, and Fleishman (2000). The skill-based model has five elements, as depicted in Table 2.3. The focus is on capabilities, which encompass knowledge, skills, and abilities in a holistic framework, and the relationship between a leader's capabilities and their performance. These leadership capabilities are developed through a combination of both education and experience, and directly link to performance outcomes.

Table 2.3

Skill-Based Leadership Model				
Individual Attributes	Competencies	Leadership Outcomes	Career Experiences	Environmental Influences
Cognitive Ability	Problem Solving Skills	Performance	Job Assignments and Roles	Internal Factors
Motivation	Social Judgment Skills	Solutions From Effective Problem Solving	Mentoring and Coaching	External Factors
Personality Traits	Knowledge		Training and Development	

(Mumford, Zaccaro, Harding, et al., 2000)

Each of these five unique elements represents a critical contributing factor for leading effectively. No one element exists on its own, but rather they combine and align for impactful leadership with measurable results. This model can be relevant and beneficial for many organizations as part of a leadership development strategy, through the clear and tangible mapping of individual strengths, KSA gaps, and areas for development. All of the elements in the model can be examined as part of a needs assessment for one or more individuals, which can be used to build targeted training and development programs with specific learning outcomes and capability goals.

An important consideration in applying these different KSA models to real-world scenarios is the importance of an ongoing needs assessment to determine which areas may need additional emphasis at any given time. This is often referred to as 'taking the pulse' of a situation. A proactive leader will regularly assess all of the known internal and external factors and forces that could impact the organization's workforce, its processes and operations, and the future sustainability of its products and services.

To conclude this chapter, a leader's unique combination of traits is not one-size-fits-all with regard to all circumstances and needs, and must be relevant to the setting and context in which the leader is functioning. Lastly, the importance and value of a leader's traits is contingent on how well those traits enable the leader to build and leverage their KSA's to demonstrate the behaviors needed to perform appropriately and produce outcomes. All of these elements should fit together like pieces of a puzzle, and the finished puzzle is the end goal or objective.

Chapter Summary

◆ A positive and impactful leader must possess a diverse array of attributes, including personal traits and characteristics, areas of knowledge and expertise, skills, and abilities that support an effective partnership with their followers and the fulfillment of their vision and mission.

◆ Trait studies have provided a valuable component for research on leadership that yielded significant findings regarding the impact and importance of specific traits and characteristics on effective leader performance and outcomes.

◆ A leader's traits must be relevant to the setting and context in which they are performing, and their effectiveness depends on how well those traits enable them to apply their knowledge, skills, and abilities (KSA's) to demonstrate the behaviors needed for high performance and outcomes.

◆ Research findings on leadership knowledge, skills, and capabilities produced unique but equally important skill categories including technical skills, human skills, and conceptual skills. This research emphasized the alignment between leader traits and KSA's in conjunction with their experience, and generated focus on the idea that leadership could be developed through proper education, skill-building, and coaching, resulting in the achievement of desired performance outcomes.

Quiz 2

1. A leader who demonstrates a willingness to seek input from creative and forward-thinking minds within an organization, and take reasonable risks to develop innovative ideas into new products, is most likely demonstrating which Big Five personality trait?

   a. Conscientiousness

   b. Openness to Experience

   c. Agreeableness

   d. Emotional Stability

2. A leader that can see a situation through the lens or perspective of their followers, even if it's quite different from their own perception of a situation, is likely demonstrating which component of emotional intelligence?

   a. Self-awareness

   b. Relationship management

   c. Social awareness

   d. Self-management

3. **A leader who communicates truthfully and with transparency most likely possesses which of the following universally positive leader attributes, as identified through research from the GLOBE Project?**

   a. Intelligent

   b. Honest

   c. Decisive

   d. Motivational

4. **The area of mentoring and coaching is integrated into which of the categories of the Skill-based Leadership Model?**

   a. Environmental Influences

   b. Competencies

   c. Leadership Outcomes

   d. Career Experiences

5. An organizational leader who regularly assesses external
    trends and influencing factors in relation to economic shifts
    and consumer spending to determine patterns for forecasting
    and long-term planning is applying which skill set?

    a. Interpersonal skills

    b. Technical skills

    c. Conceptual skills

    d. Decision making skills

Solutions to the above questions can be downloaded from
the **Online Resources** *section of this book on*
www.vibrantpublishers.com

Chapter 3

Leadership Behavior

As we explored in the previous chapter, a leader's unique combination of attributes, comprised of their traits, knowledge, skills, and abilities, are critically important in terms of how effective they are and the extent to which they successfully achieve goals towards a desired vision and mission. That said, leadership attributes do not tell the whole story. These attributes should enable a leader to think and behave in ways that facilitate performance expectations, attain goals and objectives, and drive positive results and outcomes. A leader's attributes alone do not provide the measurable results needed to achieve a vision – they must facilitate relevant behaviors, which in turn provide those desired results. Leadership attributes and behaviors should fit together like a key in a lock that opens a critically important door to fulfilling a vision and mission.

In this chapter, our focus is on the array of behaviors that impact the leader-follower partnership as well as potentially affect their goal achievement and progress. We will examine the relevant theories, concepts, and models that comprise the behavioral approach to leadership, and their application in real-world scenarios.

After reading this chapter, key learning objectives attained will include:

- Understanding the alignment between a leader's attributes and their demonstrated behaviors.

- Explaining key findings from foundational research on leadership behavior.

- Describing examples that comprise both the interpersonal relationship-focused and the task/ production-focused dimensions of leader behavior.

- Analyzing different leadership styles and the positive and negative implications of each style for achieving and sustaining a harmonious, collaborative, trusting climate for the group that facilitates task completion, strong performance, and goal attainment.

3.1 Pioneering Research on Leader Behavioral Theory

The study of leadership behaviors and their impact on a leader's effectiveness emerged primarily from mid-20th century research efforts that laid the groundwork for an expansion of a more sophisticated and dynamic understanding of behavioral leadership approaches and styles: the Ohio State University studies and the University of Michigan studies.

3.1.1 The Ohio State University Studies

Occurring in the late 1940's, the Ohio State University studies were based on Stogdill's (1948) findings that posited the importance of leader behaviors as a complementary element to their traits. Researchers developed a list of 1800 leader behaviors which was further narrowed down, categorized, and organized into 150 items representing key leadership functions and leader behaviors. The resulting categories that emerged were named consideration and initiating structure (Yukl, 1998).

Consideration represents any behaviors related to taking care of the individuals involved in some manner with the leader and their vision, such as employees, customers, and the community. Initiating structure represents the action-oriented behaviors needed to perform any activities and functions to achieve the goals and outcomes needed for the leader's vision. The behaviors that encompass each dimension are described in Table 3.1.

Table 3.1

Consideration	Initiating Structure
Building positive relationships with individuals through authenticity and rapport	Building an environment that encourages and recognizes individual and group performance and productivity
Creating a climate of trust through honest and transparent communication	Clearly articulating goals and objectives, and defining clear roles and assigning them to the appropriate individuals
Demonstrating respect for others through non-judgmental feedback, support, and validation	Specifying tasks and timelines, and delegating tasks and activities to followers or group members with clear directions and a detailed explanation for expectations of performance outcomes

Consideration	Initiating Structure
Being accessible/visible, approachable, and accommodating to the group's needs and concerns	Maintaining ongoing and open communication channels, formal and informal, including meetings, calls, check-ins, reminders, and emails/written communication, and offering updates as needed in a timely manner
Motivating followers through inspiration and positive, encouraging, forward-thinking messaging and attitude	Offering adequate resources and instructions for followers or group members to accomplish their respective tasks with ease
Facilitating a harmonious and cohesive connection among followers or group members to interact with cooperation, empathy, and mutual respect	Seeking appropriate input from followers or group members on planning out tasks and work aligned with timeline, due dates, and scheduling, as well as meeting agenda items and updates
Encouraging cooperation and collaboration by working together, sharing resources, and relying on each other for achieving collective goals and objectives	Setting realistic and tangible goals, ensuring that everyone has a reasonable balance of work load in terms of complexity and quantity of output
Developing followers in a manner that enables them to feel valued, taken care of, and invested in for their own growth and fulfillment	Providing constructive feedback to individual followers to reinforce desired performance behaviors and offering guidance to improve areas of knowledge and skill gaps
Providing emotional support, coaching, guidance, and encouragement, based on a leader's best assessment of the specific needs of each follower or group member at any given time	Communicating productivity and performance updates to individuals and group, sharing goals attained, emphasizing where goals have not been met and how to focus in order to achieve them in a timely manner
Promoting shared values and acting as a role model and example of those values on a daily basis, as well as recognizing group members when they demonstrate shared values in their own different and unique ways	Aligning followers or group members so everyone is moving in the same direction towards the shared mission, even though their respective individual tasks and activities are different from one another

The Ohio State University studies provided important insights into how leader behaviors resonate with their followers with varying needs and/or in different situations. For example, one follower or group member may need validation that their knowledge and skills are needed to help fulfill their mission. Another may seek recognition for their efforts and feel valued and appreciated. Yet another may seek challenging goals and opportunities to grow to their fullest potential.

Additionally, these findings demonstrated the importance of the relationship between a leader's behaviors and the performance outcomes for themselves and their followers. An appropriate balance of leader behaviors is critical to sustaining positive, collaborative relationships among everyone involved as well as maintaining productivity, quality output and effectiveness. For example, a leader with low consideration behaviors and high initiating structure behaviors may ensure productivity and adherence to deadlines, but morale and motivation may be lacking. Conversely, a leader with high consideration and low initiating structure may foster a cohesive, trusting, and fun climate, but performance and productivity may not be as focused as it needs to be to produce quality and timely outcomes. That said, the needs of the followers or group may shift based on various influencing factors, requiring the leader to assess needs regularly and adjust their behaviors accordingly. For example, a team that is going through a conflict will most likely not be productive until the issue is resolved and harmony is restored. Therefore, a leader may need to focus and emphasize consideration behaviors until the team is trusting and collaborative once again, and then pivot back into task and performance outcomes mode. Based on these examples, it is clear that leader behaviors are not one-size-fits-all, and are also not static – they need to shift and adapt all the time, and an effective leader needs to be able to (1) assess needs and circumstances on an ongoing basis, and (2) understand which behaviors are needed when and how to adjust their actions appropriately.

The Ohio State University studies set a sound and relevant foundation for the further examination of dimensions of leader behaviors and the extent of their effectiveness when demonstrated in different types of situations with diverse followers or group members. Around the same time period that this research was being conducted, similar research studies were occurring at the University of Michigan.

3.1.2 The University of Michigan Studies

Following the trailblazing behavioral findings from the Ohio State University researchers, the University of Michigan studies emerged shortly thereafter. The focus of this research was also on leader performance and effectiveness based on an array of key behaviors. Leveraging the findings from Ohio State, the University of Michigan researchers sought to validate and expand upon the relevance and importance of the behavioral categories of consideration and initiating structure. The findings from the University of Michigan studies produced two behavioral dimensions of leadership that aligned well with the consideration and initiating structure, referred to as relationship-orientation and task/production-orientation (Yukl, 1998).

A relationship-oriented leader is focused on the needs of their followers or group members. These leaders provide a positive and respectful environment, ensure their followers are well-supported and their needs are met, are responsive and honest communicators, seek to inspire and motivate their followers, build rapport and trust between themselves and their followers as well as among each other, act as a coach and trusted adviser, and emphasize each follower or group member's role as a valued contributor (Bowers & Seashore, 1966). Relationship-oriented leader behaviors are similar to the consideration dimension of the Ohio State University study findings, with emphasis on fostering positive interactions between the leader and their followers or group members to sustain a mutually beneficial relationship.

A task/production-oriented leader will demonstrate behaviors that are in alignment with the initiating structure dimension of the Ohio State University study findings. Typical behaviors that comprise a task and production focus include:

- Setting goals, planning, and organizing work tasks and schedules

- Assigning roles to individuals, delegating activities based on role, explaining performance outcomes and expectations, providing training and adequate resources for performance and output

- Communicating regularly through an array of modalities.

- Analyzing data through key metrics to assess outcomes such as quality, efficiency, production, and goal achievement.

In addition to the relationship and task/production behavioral dimensions, University of Michigan researchers also examined a third type of behavior that impacted leader performance, referred to as participative leadership (Yukl, 1998). The concept of participative leadership is based on a strategic integration of behaviors that promote and support shared participation in the context of both of the other two dimensions, relationship-orientation and task/production-orientation. Depending on the situation and set of circumstances, the leader will empower their followers or group members to contribute and offer input towards a variety of goals and needs. In the context of supporting relationship building, a participative leader will share opportunities for collaboration, recognition, conflict resolution, and team building with the group. In the context of promoting task and production focus, a participative leader may share goal setting, creating tasks and schedules, problem solving, brainstorming, and decision making with their group members.

The practice of participative leadership may be particularly beneficial when a group is geographically dispersed, working on different shifts, or in different environments. Group members are in sync with the leader and with each other, and the leader can rely on followers' alignment with their goals and the needs of the entire group, allowing everyone to make valuable contributions. In this way, a leader leverages all that their group members may have to offer to serve the collective effort and to support the leader so they do not have to be 'everything to everybody' all the time. Of course, a leader integrating participative behaviors must still be mindful of areas in which they may still need to lead on their own without sharing the effort with their followers or group members. Every situation must be carefully assessed, including any time-related constraints and need for urgency, level of relevant expertise among group members, and extent to which a task or need is too sensitive or risky for shared input. We will examine this practice in the context of team leadership a bit further in this book.

Both the Ohio State University and the University of Michigan studies have provided a critical cornerstone for behavioral theories, models, and applications to develop. The organization of leader behaviors into distinct dimensions has been successfully leveraged and applied in an array of conditions and contexts. Practical tools and resources have been created using these behavioral models and classification systems for such needs as leadership training and development, management coaching, and performance evaluation and assessment of effectiveness. In the next section, we will examine a well-known leadership development tool that has been successfully integrated into managerial and leadership coaching programs for many years and continues to be a respected and relevant resource today, the Managerial (Leadership) Grid (Blake & Mouton, 1964).

3.2 The Managerial (Leadership) Grid®

The Managerial Grid®, developed by researchers Blake and Mouton (1964), was designed by leveraging the aforementioned behavioral research findings relevant to managers of all levels and functions for use as a constructive, developmental tool. Also referred to as the Leadership Grid and the Managerial-Leadership Grid, it has been used successfully by organizations in the areas of leadership selection, performance management, and training and development. This tool has demonstrated effectiveness and utility for years, and continues to be relevant and highly applicable among an array of industries, settings, and context.

The Managerial (Leadership) Grid® graphically depicts managerial/leadership behavior based on two behavioral dimensions: concern for people and concern for production. The concern for people dimension focuses on interpersonal relationships, camaraderie, trust, and respect. On the other hand, the concern for production dimension focuses on tasks, performance, and results. A manager's leadership behaviors can be assessed and scored as low (1) - to moderate (5) - up to high (9) - on both of these dimensions. As depicted in Figure 3.1, the horizontal axis represents the concern for production dimension and the vertical axis represents the concern for people dimension.

The grid is comprised of five different categories of leadership style, based on different combinations of behaviors along these two axes:

- **Impoverished Management (1, 1)**

  - low on both concern for people and concern for production

- **Country Club Management (1, 9)**

  - low on concern for production and high on concern for people

- **Authority-Compliance Management (9, 1)**

  - high on concern for production and low on concern for people

- **Team Management (9, 9)**

  - high on both concern for people and concern for production

- **Middle-of-the-Road Management (5, 5)**

  - moderate on both concern for people and concern for production

(Blake & Mouton, 1964)

Figure 3.1

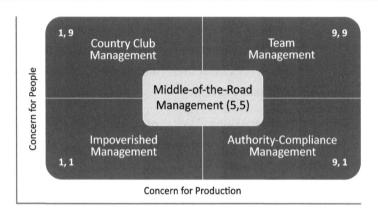

By working with the Managerial (Leadership) Grid®, along with other assessment instruments and behavioral inventories, an organization can examine a manager's behaviors and 'go-to' tendencies to assess their leadership style for evaluating their performance and identifying not only skill deficits and areas for improvement, but also best practices for sharing and mentoring. In the next section, we will conclude this chapter with some relevant examples of behavioral best practices among effective leaders.

3.3 Behavioral Best Practices of Effective Leaders

Imagine you could interview a leader that you admire, past or present. What would you ask them about their preferences and tactics for behaving in the most productive, collaborative, and impactful manner possible, fulfilling both person/relationship and task/goal-oriented needs simultaneously? What would you expect that leader to share with you as their best practices? Leaders, both formal and informal, should consider the behaviors and approaches below as they continue to develop their own unique leadership style that serves both their followers/group members as well as the goals and tasks at hand:

- Start each day by asking, "What needs to be done?" to maintain task and work completion milestones, and follow up by asking, "What can I/we do to make a difference?" to maintain focus on the vision.

- Understand the needs, concerns, and challenges of followers or group members by being approachable and accessible, and maintaining open two-way lines of communication for both listening and sharing information.

- Create a climate of inclusion and respect by valuing diversity among followers or group members, appreciating the strengths of individual differences, and encouraging employees to be their unique selves.

- Clearly prioritize goals and their required task needs, aligning with realistic and tangible results, and making adjustments as necessary.

- Ensure the current vision and mission continue to be relevant amid shifting trends and needs, make modifications to adapt accordingly, and share with followers or group members to ensure everyone is in sync with short and long-term goals and expected outcomes.

- Stay accountable for the performance and outcomes of the entire group or organization and take responsibility for any issues that arise – as a leader, nothing is never not 'their' fault.

- Sustain self-awareness to behave with integrity and objectivity, demonstrate a strong work ethic, and act as a consistent role model with which followers or group members can resonate.

An effective leader will recognize the need for a balance of all of the behaviors within these dimensions and be able to apply their unique attributes to act in a manner that facilitates performance, enables goal achievement, and also serves the needs of their followers. In addition, a strong leader will understand how to assess a situation and its distinct contextual factors in an effort to implement the most appropriate balance of task-focused and interpersonal relationship-focused behaviors needed, which is the focus of our next chapter.

Chapter Summary

◆ A leader's unique combination of attributes should enable them to think and behave in ways that facilitate the follower's motivations to perform collaboratively and productively, enable the attainment of goals and objectives, and drive positive results and outcomes.

◆ Early research from Ohio State University provided key insight into two main categories of leadership behaviors: consideration and initiating structure, the former focused on interpersonal relationships with followers, and the latter focused on work and task completion and performance.

◆ Subsequent research from the University of Michigan offered validation to the results obtained from the Ohio State University studies, and further explored these behaviors in the context of two dimensions referred to as relationship-orientation and task/production-orientation.

◆ A valuable leadership assessment and development tool still used today is the Managerial (Leadership) Grid, developed by Blake and Mouton in 1964, which organizes leader behavior into five styles based on low-moderate-high levels of two dimensions referred to as concern for people and concern for production.

Quiz 3

1. **Which of the following leader behaviors would be considered part of the consideration behavioral dimension?**

   a. Setting relevant goals and objectives and their associated required tasks

   b. Offering recognition and appreciation for excellent performance and effort

   c. Assigning clear and relevant roles to group members

   d. Offering training and development opportunities to address knowledge and skill needs

2. **Which of the following leader behaviors would be considered part of the initiating structure behavioral dimension?**

   a. Creating enthusiasm among members for the team's mission and values

   b. Offering opportunities for team members to approach the leader with questions

   c. Coordinating weekly meetings and setting an agenda

   d. Building rapport and trust among new members

3. **The behavioral dimension referred to as the initiating structure that emerged from the Ohio State University studies is most closely aligned with which behavioral dimension produced by the University of Michigan studies?**

   a. Concern for People

   b. Task Management

   c. Task/Production Orientation

   d. Initiating Process

4. **A leader that demonstrates a high level of concern and care for their followers/group members as well as a high level of task-orientation and focus on performance would most likely fall into which leadership style on the Managerial (Leadership) Grid?**

   a. Authority-Compliance Management

   b. Country Club Management

   c. Impoverished Management

   d. Team Management

5. According to the Managerial (Leadership) Grid, a manager who creates an inclusive, trusting, and harmonious group environment, but does not focus on setting goals, delegating tasks, or adhering to deadlines and expectations, would likely fall into which leadership style?

   a. Authority-Compliance Management

   b. Country Club Management

   c. Middle-of-the-Road Management

   d. Team Management

Solutions to the above questions can be downloaded from
the **Online Resources** *section of this book on*
www.vibrantpublishers.com

This page is intentionally left blank

Chapter 4

Situational and Contingency Leadership

While an array of leadership best practices and approaches do exist for leaders and managers to successfully implement with their respective group and setting, there is no single answer or formula for being an impactful leader in every situation and context. Different situations will require different leadership styles and as needs and circumstances vary and shift, a leader must adapt their behaviors accordingly to meet those changing needs and expectations. An effective leader will have an awareness of internal and external factors that influence changing circumstances, and understand how to apply their traits, knowledge, skills, and abilities to act in a relevant and appropriate manner in response to the unique requirements and demands of a particular situation. This understanding comes from leadership education and development, experience leading in various contexts and settings, and a bit of practice and patience.

In this chapter, we will examine key theories, models, and tools for developing situational leadership awareness and skill-based competency.

After reading this chapter, key learning objectives attained will include:

- Understanding the impact of different types of situations, internal and external influences, and planned/unplanned circumstances that may necessitate different leader behaviors and styles.

- Explaining the key findings of situational and contingency leadership research that continue to be applied among today's organizations and institutions.

- Describing the similarities and differences of foundational situational and contingency leadership theories, concepts, and models.

- Analyzing followers' needs along with the contextual factors of a situation to determine the most appropriate combination of leader behaviors for a strategic approach that serves those needs, satisfies unique situational requirements, and facilitates performance and goal attainment.

4.1 Factors Influencing Leadership Style

As we have examined, a leader's role in any situation is part of a complex system with internal and external factors affecting the circumstances, and ultimately performance outcomes for the leader and their group.

> The consensus among the most respected researchers in the area of situational leadership suggests that leadership style and approach depends on several key factors:
>
> - The leader's attributes and style.
>
> - The situation – internal and external factors.
>
> - The goals and tasks that need to be performed.
>
> - The characteristics of the leader's followers.

(The Peter F. Drucker Foundation, 1996)

Additionally, different leader behaviors and strategies are necessary at various stages of group or organizational development. In the start-up phase, a situation may require focus in establishing a vision and mission, gaining exposure, and generating enthusiasm. Moving into the growth phase, a situation may call for developing a strategy, establishing core values and principles, planning short and long-term goals and objectives, and creating roles for members. As the group or organization progresses, there may be situations that emerge of varying degrees of change, re-assessment, crisis, and success. To that end, it is important for leaders to have the knowledge, skills, and tools to competently navigate a group through diverse situations and changing needs, sometimes well out of their own comfort zone. In the following sections, we will examine several foundational theories and models of situational and contingency-based leadership.

4.2 Fiedler's Contingency Theory

The research of Fred Fiedler in the area of situational and contingency leadership is widely recognized and respected, conducted largely through working with an array of groups directed by a formal leader in a structured leadership role. Fiedler surmised that effective leadership is not solely the result of a leader's attributes, nor is it exclusively based on the nature of the situation. Fiedler proposed that a leader's effectiveness is contingent on both their attributes/leadership style and the level of control they have over the current situation. Moreover, the level of situational control is dependent on (1) leader-member relations; (2) task structure including clarity of goals, roles, tasks, and expectations; and (3) legitimate position power and scope of group authority (Fiedler, 1964).

Fiedler and his colleagues developed an assessment tool called the Least Preferred Co-worker (LPC) scale. This instrument was designed to measure the extent to which a leader describes the co-worker with whom they work the least well as either favorably or unfavorably. Leaders consider their least preferred co-worker and rate that individual on a variety of attributes such as pleasant-unpleasant, rejecting-accepting, supportive-hostile, trustworthy-untrustworthy, and boring-interesting. A leader that rates their least preferred co-worker in a fairly favorable manner would be considered a more interpersonal relationship-oriented leader, while a more task/performance-oriented leader would likely rate their least preferred co-worker in less favorable terms (Fiedler, Chemers, & Mahar, 1976). This knowledge is valuable for leadership development and coaching in terms of addressing areas of need to facilitate leader self-awareness and adaptability/responsiveness to different situations.

While their findings support the idea that a leader's style can be flexible in response to changing needs and conditions, Fiedler and his colleagues have also proposed that leadership style is still fairly stable, similar to one's personality traits. It is not realistic to expect that a leader who directs well in an area that is relatively low-risk, focused, and routine will be able to constantly pivot and perform just as well in situations of dramatically varying degrees of risk, uncertainty, task requirements, and urgency. An organization should strive to align leaders with the setting, context, and performance expectations that are best suited to their predominant style, and provide coaching to improve their agility and adaptability when changing conditions arise.

4.3 Path-Goal Theory

Just as leaders need to find the most suitable balance of task and interpersonal relationship focus to be most effective in a given situation, they should also determine the best approach for clarifying the path to goal achievement. The path-goal theory, developed by Robert House (1971) offers insight for enabling a leader to motivate their followers or group members to achieve specific goals. By defining goals, clarifying a path, removing obstacles, and providing support, a leader can facilitate competent and streamlined task completion for their group members. These supportive behaviors will sufficiently motivate and fulfill needs, resulting in group member satisfaction and engagement, desired performance, and goal achievement (Northouse, 2016).

Followers or group members need to understand the outcomes that result from performing the tasks and activities necessary in their respective roles, and how those outcomes will benefit them as well as the leader and the group and/or organization. Followers also need to personally resonate with the goals in order to be fully invested and apply their knowledge, skills, and abilities to their highest potential. This is a clear example of the power of 'WIIFM', or 'What's In It For Me'. Each follower needs to have their own unique WIIFM needs addressed in a clear and appealing way, otherwise they may not understand how they will individually benefit from contributing which can result in a lack of acceptance and motivation to perform. Additionally, the path represents the process. A leader should make the path from the effort/work to the outcome as tangible and straightforward as possible, providing clear directions, resources, and expectations and removing obstacles and challenges as best as possible (House, 1971; House & Mitchell, 1974).

The impact of the path-goal theory on leadership effectiveness is dependent on (1) situational variables comprised of task characteristics and follower characteristics; (2) follower motivation and expectation; and (3) leader behavior. The theory supports four main types of leader behavior:

1. Supportive

- Leader is approachable and accessible, making time for members as needed.

- Leader provides guidance, encouragement, and coaching.

- Leader creates a comfortable and inclusive environment.

2. Directive

- Leader assigns roles to members that are appropriate and clearly defined.

- Leader provides realistic tasks with detailed instructions and timeline.

- Leader provides resources and materials that members will need to perform tasks.

- Leader sets tangible goals and explains their performance expectations.

3. Participative

- Leader shares decision making with group members.

- Leader encourages members to share their feedback, perspectives, and ideas.

- Leader ensures that all members have opportunities to offer input.

4. Achievement-oriented

- Leader has high standards that are communicated to the group in terms of clearly defined goals and outcomes.

- Leader helps group members develop their confidence and sense of self-efficacy.

- Leader offers opportunities for members to challenge themselves through elevated goals as appropriate.

Path-goal theory suggests that a leader should identify the combination of behaviors from one or more of these areas most appropriate and relevant to each follower, and a leader may actively demonstrate different behaviors towards different followers simultaneously. For example, one group member may be ready for a new challenging project to give them a little push towards a high-level goal, while another group member may be new in their role and need clear directions and expectations to be in sync with the leader. Leaders must be aware of what their followers need to stay motivated and perform their roles with confidence, competence, clarity, and ease as they progress towards achieving goals.

4.4 Situational Leadership Theory

Aligned with the pioneering work of Fiedler, House, and their colleagues, researchers Hersey and Blanchard (1969, 1977) also made important contributions in the area of situational leadership. They developed the Situational Leadership Model, a functional tool for leadership development that is still relevant and used today in many organizations. The model consists of a directive dimension and a supportive dimension, and illustrates how a leader should integrate each appropriately after assessing a particular situation and its needs. Behaviors associated with the directive dimension are task-oriented and focus on productivity, goal attainment, and performance. Behaviors associated with the supportive dimension are interpersonal relationship-focused and emphasize open communication, trust, cooperation, and recognition.

According to Hersey and Blanchard, follower needs in varying circumstances will impact a leader's balance of directive and supportive behaviors. Specifically, their level of competence and commitment should be determining factors when deciding on a leadership approach. Different situations will impact followers' commitment and competence levels in different ways. Think about it – are you fully skilled, competent, and invested in every type of academic or work situation? Most (if not all) of us probably could not answer yes to this question. Ideally, a leader should recognize the needs and drivers of their followers or group members in different situations, and adjust their own behaviors to meet them appropriately. Even though this leadership strategy may sound as if the leader is simply catering to their followers, it is a two-way exchange. When follower/group member needs are identified and fulfilled, they will be able to support the leader's goals and objectives through task completion and performance in their respective roles.

In 1985, Blanchard developed the Situational Leadership II (SLII®) Model which provides four categories of leadership styles based on different low-high combinations of the directive and supportive dimensions:

S1: High Directive/Low Supportive ⇨ Directing Style

- The S1 leadership style may be implemented when the focus needs to be on delegating tasks, providing clear and specific instructions, and staying engaged with followers to ensure work completion and desired performance outcomes. Supportive behaviors exist, but are minimized to avoid creating too friendly and familiar of a rapport when productivity is the priority.

S2: High Directive/High Supportive ⇨ Coaching Style

- The S2 leadership style may be used when task/work output as well as interpersonal needs are both equally high. Consider a work environment following a layoff or disruption. Morale would likely be low, but performance is still essential to keep the organization moving forward. A leader would have to demonstrate behaviors in both dimensions simultaneously, while staying aware of changing follower needs.

S3: Low Directive/High Supportive ⇨ Supporting Style

- The S3 leadership style may be appropriate when followers need more input from the leader in terms of inspiration, motivation, and confidence. The leader may decide to focus less on delegating, planning work, and influencing performance and outcomes, empowering followers or group members to manage those needs appropriately among themselves.

S4: Low Directive/Low Supportive ⇨ Delegating Style

- The S4 leadership style may be employed when the group is fully capable, functional, and invested, requiring little input and oversight from the leader. Followers understand the goals, their respective roles and tasks, and the leader's expectations. They are also able to work together collaboratively and harmoniously, and do not need extensive motivation and interpersonal support from the leader.

While these leadership styles can be helpful for leaders in terms of understanding the behaviors and actions they should demonstrate to serve the needs of their group, it is important for a leader to not remain locked into any one style, as needs will continue to shift as situations change and evolve. Using the Situational Leadership Model, a leader can assess the needs of their followers or group members and determine the best approach in a situation to meet interpersonal as well as task/goal needs and perform competently to achieve objectives.

4.5 Leader-Member Exchange (LMX) Theory

A focus on the interactive exchange dynamic between a leader and their followers also forms the basis of the leader-member exchange (LMX) theory. A leader will develop a unique exchange with each follower or group member in which the follower provides output or a needed deliverable to the leader and in return, the leader provides the follower with a desired outcome or response. As a follower provides more in terms of quality, quantity, and/or goes above and beyond their role to serve the group's mission and goals, the leader will respond accordingly with a greater return in exchange. Their response may include reward and recognition, access to more or certain types of resources, increased decision-making ability, increased autonomy, project/task preference, and increased level of responsibility (Forsyth, 2010). Followers or group members that maintain status quo, performing their assigned tasks at an average level of performance and not extending themselves beyond the prescribed scope of their role, will continue to receive a more typical, basic exchange from the leader in return for their effort.

Research (Dansereau, Graen, & Haga, 1975) examining leader-follower exchange relationship dynamics provided insights regarding two types of follower relationships, the in-group and the out-group:

In-group/Leader Dynamics

- Members are highly involved, invested, and engaged, willing to go beyond their respective roles to support the leader and to drive positive results.

- In exchange for this higher level of effort and commitment, the leader will provide these group members with an array of benefits and perks (as described in the above section) that may be appealing and sustain their motivation to continue to engage in this manner.

- This relationship provides for the needs of a leader's high-level performers and empowers them to rise to their fullest potential with the knowledge and validation that their efforts are recognized, valued, and will continue to be rewarded appropriately.

Out-group/Leader Dynamics

- Members demonstrate fair to average involvement and engagement, and their expectations are minimal.

- Out-group members are more inclined to follow the scope of their role and perform their tasks and duties as directed; they 'do what they need to do' and that's all.

- They are not necessarily poor performers, but they do not wish to expand their contributions and efforts beyond the capacity of their role to serve the collective goals in a bigger way.

- The leader does provide them with an exchange of benefits for their output, but not to the extent of what the in-group receives.

Ideally, out-group members will observe the exchange between the leader and the in-group members and find it appealing enough that they shift their behaviors, raise the bar on their own performance, and strive to move into the in-group. LMX theory does not suggest that a leader maintains a type of exclusionary 'club' in which the out-group members are shut out of any type of exchange. Members who are part of the out-group at any given time are still supported and treated fairly and with respect, but members of the in-group will receive more from the leader in terms of investment because of their consistently exemplary contributions and dedication that goes beyond themselves in their contained role, for the greater good and benefit of the group and the organization. In exchange, the leader will support their needs in a greater capacity for growth and continued engagement.

The leader will establish a baseline of appropriate exchanges for follower or group member performance and productivity, and those who demonstrate behaviors that go above that baseline will receive enhanced and more desirable exchange offerings from the leader in return.

There is no bias or favoritism implied in the LMX theory, though it is strongly recommended to exercise caution when making high-stakes decisions such as a pay raise or job promotion in response to in-group member performance, when a leader may be guilty of neglecting out-group member needs and allowing them to fall behind without any outreach or appropriate coaching. Additionally, a leader should continuously observe member activity/inactivity to assess any out-group behaviors and determine (1) why they are occurring and (2) how to encourage and motivate those members. A leader should always provide a certain standard of exchange to all followers or group members, and be vigilant in identifying shifts in engagement levels, effort, and involvement in order to adjust their own approach to fulfill changing member needs.

Membership in the in-group and the out-group may also be somewhat fluid in which an in-group member fades into the background for a period of time for a particular reason (e.g., personal issue taking priority), moves into the out-group for a while, and eventually returns to the in-group. Conversely, an out-group member may decide that the extra effort and engagement needed to be part of the in-group is worth it based on the demonstrated exchange between the leader and in-group members. The out-group member may then be motivated to contribute and perform at a higher level consistently enough for the leader to invest in and provide for them as an in-group member.

Subsequent research examined the impact of the different types of leader-member exchange relationships on leader effectiveness, follower/group member job satisfaction and performance, and desired results for the group as well as the organization as a whole. Research findings have demonstrated that quality, mutually beneficial exchanges between a leader and their followers can result in the following positive outcomes:

- Increased job satisfaction, group member engagement, commitment, and positive attitudes.

- Increased group member performance.

- Improved role clarity and expectations, resulting in greater likelihood of personal advancement.

- Increased leader effectiveness in both productivity/goal attainment and group cohesion and support.

- Increased likelihood of objectives being met that drive measurable results and fulfill a higher-level purpose.

(Liden, Wayne, & Stilwell, 1993; Graen & Uhl-Bien, 1995)

LMX theory is very much a 'real world' concept, as the presence of in-group and out-group members is a likely reality in any setting. It is unrealistic to believe that all followers or members will always be fully engaged, or that a member who is disengaged one week won't shift into engagement and active contribution the next week (or vice versa). LMX theory can be applied in the design of leadership development and coaching programs, enabling current and future leaders to identify the behaviors of out-group members and hone their awareness of their needs and challenges. This ongoing awareness is the key to understanding how to engage different group members by acknowledging and fulfilling their unique needs through positive rapport, open communication, and an array of tailored approaches and best practices. LMX theory supports the idea that an interactive exchange relationship is the foundation for effective leadership as a process and not merely a set of actions that the leader performs on their own in a vacuum. This dynamic relationship is necessary to build a sound partnership between a leader and their followers, and is critical to achieving desired and necessary outcomes and making progress in the fulfillment of the group or organization's mission and vision.

The concepts, theories, and models covered in this chapter illustrate the value and importance of accurately assessing situational and contextual elements when determining an appropriate leadership approach, including but not limited to influencing factors such as:

- Leader-member relations

- Task type, structure, and complexity

- Follower/group member attributes and needs

- Follower/group member commitment and engagement

- Leader position and type/extent of control

- Group climate, dynamics, and norms

- Expected performance outcomes and goal type/timeline

- External influences and stakeholder expectations

- Presence of risk/crisis circumstances

It is important to remember that no theory or model is perfect. While there are similarities and themes among them, each has its own valuable contributions that may be more or less relevant to leaders in certain types of environs. The situational and contingency leadership style is comprised of constructive, practical tools and techniques to integrate with trait/attribute-based and behavioral-based approaches for a holistic leadership strategy.

Chapter Summary

♦ Different situations will require different leadership styles, and as needs and circumstances vary and shift, a leader must adapt their behaviors accordingly to meet those changing needs and expectations.

♦ Fiedler's contingency theory posits that effective leadership is not solely the result of a leader's attributes or solely the nature of a situation, but rather contingent on a combination of their attributes/leadership style and the level of control they have over the current situation comprised of leader-member relations, task structure, and position power.

♦ House's path-goal theory provides insight for enabling a leader to motivate their followers to achieve specific and clearly defined goals through behaviors such as clarifying a path, removing obstacles, and providing support. Through this approach, a leader can facilitate task completion for their followers, resulting in engagement, desired performance, and goal achievement.

♦ Researchers Hersey and Blanchard created the Situational Leadership Model to accurately assess different situations and needs, consisting of a directive dimension and a supportive dimension. Followers' needs in varying circumstances as well as their level of competence and commitment will impact a leader's balance of directive and supportive behaviors.

◆ Leader-member exchange (LMX) theory emphasizes a dynamic exchange relationship between leader and followers. Followers demonstrating greater engagement and contribution who perform above and beyond their roles to serve the group are referred to as the in-group, and followers who perform satisfactorily without greater involvement and interest are referred to as the out-group. A leader may offer enhanced attention, resources, and investment in the in-group members in exchange.

Quiz 4

1. All of the following are influencing factors included in Fiedler's contingency theory of leadership, with the exception of_____.

   a. followers' knowledge and skills

   b. leader-member relations

   c. task structure

   d. position power

2. In most situations, unless there are strong indicators of a particular need, a leader should strive to focus on _____.

   a. relationships more than tasks

   b. tasks more than relationships

   c. a balance of tasks and relationships

   d. goal setting and discipline

3. According to the LPC scale, a leader's description of their _____ is an accurate indicator of their task or interpersonal relationship orientation.

   a. likely preferred co-worker

   b. lowest performing co-worker

   c. lowest priority co-worker

   d. least preferred co-worker

4. The leader-member exchange (LMX) theory proposes that a leader will have group members that comprise an _____, demonstrating exemplary performance, involvement and engagement, and willingness to contribute in a manner that goes above and beyond the scope of their role.

   a. in-group

   b. it-group

   c. input-group

   d. inclusion-group

5. According to the Situational Leadership II (SLII®) Model, a leader should most likely implement which style to accommodate group members who need a boost of inspiration, motivation, and greater sense of confidence?

   a. S1: Directing Style

   b. S2: Coaching Style

   c. S3: Supporting Style

   d. S4: Delegating Style

Solutions to the above questions can be downloaded from the **Online Resources** *section of this book on* **www.vibrantpublishers.com**

Chapter 5

Power and Influence

In addition to the various facets of effective leadership that we have explored so far, two integral elements built into the foundation of leadership are power and influence. Power and influence are essential components to a leader's success in terms of ensuring performance and goal accomplishment as well as sustaining investment and commitment from followers or organizational group members. Ideally, all followers would be consistently on board and in alignment with their leader's vision, beliefs, values, expectations, and goals. The reality is that this sustained level of acceptance and support does not always occur naturally or easily, or without occasional challenges. In response, a leader or manager should have the ability to responsibly exert the control and persuasion necessary to appropriately and respectfully redirect group members back to their purpose and plan.

In this chapter, the concepts of power and influence will be defined individually and also described in the context of their interconnectedness. Without impactful influence approaches, any of the types of power examined in this chapter will not be adequately leveraged. Part of an effective leader's toolkit must be well-honed influence approaches, persuasive skills, and the know-how to properly use their power as well as share their power with followers.

After reading this chapter, key learning objectives attained will include:

- Defining the concepts of power and influence, and articulating the interconnected relationship between them.

- Describing the four different outcomes of power.

- Differentiating among the various types of personal power and position power.

- Comparing the different types of influence approaches and the different situations and contexts in which they may be most appropriate and useful.

- Understanding the concept of empowerment, and applying its practice to the different types of follower behaviors and actions that will enhance their level of contribution, responsibility, and investment in the shared vision and purpose of the leader.

5.1 Power and Influence Defined

Power and influence are inextricably linked and the reality is that one cannot exist without the other, in the same way that a leader cannot exist without followers. Power may be defined as the potential or capacity of an individual or group to exert control over the behaviors, beliefs, and attitudes of others to achieve desired outcomes and results. This control is referred to as influence. Influence essentially refers to the behaviors and tactics used to affect the responses of others. For an individual to have influence over one or more individuals means that they have employed specific behaviors that will offer sufficient control and persuasive ability to convince their followers to act in a desired manner. When this occurs, that individual has leveraged their power effectively.

The fascinating thing about power and influence is that everyone has some type of power. Think about a baby, completely dependent on their parents and caregivers for their every need. When a baby is uncomfortable or needs something, what do they do? That's right, the baby cries. What do the parents or caregivers do in response? They attend to the baby and take care of their immediate needs. Babies quickly learn this behavior-response pattern and understand how to obtain whatever they need day or night, as many of you may have experienced firsthand! This is power, plain and simple. While the focus is on leadership power and influence in this chapter, the purpose of this example is to illustrate the human capacity for some type and degree of power at any age and in any situation or context.

Before we examine the different types of power that an individual or leader may possess, let's first consider the different outcomes of power. It is important to recognize that power and its associated influence approaches will result in an array of different potential outcomes.

There are four main categories of power and influence outcomes, as highlighted in Table 5.1:

Table 5.1

Four Potential Outcomes of Power	
Compliance	Followers do what is asked of them by the individual or leader with power, but do not necessarily want to comply.
Identification	Followers do what is asked of them even though they may not want to, but they comply because they like and/or respect the individual or leader with power.
Internalization	Followers do what is asked of them because they support the directive and believe it is the appropriate thing to do.
Resistance	Followers do not do what is asked of them by the individual or leader with power.

These outcomes will be dependent on a variety of factors such as followers' perception of the leader, extent to which the outcome is desirable, likelihood of a negative consequence for not satisfying the directive of the leader, situational factors, and other internal and/or external influences. With this understanding of the various outcomes that many occur, let's explore the actual types of power in the next section.

5.2 Types of Power

Perhaps the most well-known and respected researchers in the area of power and influence are French and Raven (1959). Through the work of French and Raven, six categories of power emerged and are referred to as the bases of power, as described in detail below. According to French and Raven, these six bases of power fall into one of two categories: personal power and position power. Personal power is comprised of the sources of power derived from one's individual knowledge, skills, abilities, and talents. An individual can have personal power and not actually have a role of formal and structured authority, and in fact, we all have a bit of personal power to some degree in different situations. Conversely, position power is comprised of the sources of power derived from the scope of authority and control over one or more followers or a group based on the formal role, position, or title they hold. Position power is most commonly seen in professional organizations, but can also be held in a more personal context (e.g., parent, coach). An individual may have one or more of these types of power, and a leader will most certainly have multiple bases of position power and often one of more bases of personal power as well.

Personal Power

Expert power: Power based on one's expertise in a particular area; the ability to influence others through specialized knowledge, skills, or abilities

Information power: Power based on the control over pertinent and necessary information and resources others may need to access

Referent power: Power based on the respect, reverence, and admiration of others based on desirable, inspirational, and/or moral attributes

Position Power

Legitimate power: Power based on one's formal and structured role or position of authority relative to their followers or group members

Reward power: Power based on the authority and ability to give followers rewards and recognition for following directives

Coercive power: Power based on the authority and ability to manipulate or employ negative or undesirable consequences when followers do not comply with directives

(French & Raven, 1959)

While it may seem that position power is a stronger type of power and more impactful with followers, it may not support the most engaging and collaborative leader-follower relationships. By solely relying on sources of position power, a leader may have the legitimate authority to expect certain behaviors, but followers may act out of compliance rather than internalization. Personal sources of power are often seen as more effective (Kipnis, Schmidt, Swaffin-Smith, & Wilkinson, 1984) and a leader should develop their personal power sources and integrate them with their position power sources for a complementary approach that influences followers just as effectively, but in a less authoritarian manner.

Each type of power holds a unique and important benefit for a leader, enabling them to influence the attitudes, beliefs, values, and behaviors/actions of their followers or group members. There is no perfect type of power that provides all leaders in all different conditions and contexts with the same desired outcomes. Some types of power are inherent and built into a leader's role, while other types of power may be more readily and seamlessly accessible due to the unique attributes they possess. The types of power determined to be most relevant and appropriate for a leader to employ are often dependent on the type and level of support they need from followers to achieve goals and desired outcomes. This follower support will require a leader to employ different approaches to influence and persuasion which we will examine in the next section.

5.3 Influence Approaches

With a solid working knowledge of the concept of power, let's examine the behaviors and actions that an individual or leader may employ to exert or demonstrate their power. These various behaviors and actions are collectively referred to as influence. A person's influence can be leveraged to persuade others to support a particular belief or value, take a position or attitude on a topic, and adjust their own behaviors and decisions in alignment with the influential person. There are many different types of approaches to influencing others, and combining tactics is also a common strategy. Table 5.2 highlights the nine categories of influence tactics based on the research of Yukl (1989).

Table 5.2

Nine Types of Influence Tactics	
Rational Persuasion	Persuasion through the use of logical arguments and factual evidence.
Inspirational Appeals	Persuasion by appealing to followers' values, beliefs, and ideals to increase enthusiasm.
Consultation	Persuasion through seeking followers' input and contribution for planning, idea generation, and decision making, resulting in greater support and investment.
Ingratiation	Persuasion through flattery and encouraging a good mood, resulting in a favorable follower perception.
Exchange	Persuasion by exchanging favors with followers or offering a promise of benefit in return for support.
Personal Appeal	Persuasion through appeals to loyalty or friendship to followers or group members.
Coalition	Persuasion by seeking the support and assistance of others as a collective effort.
Legitimating	Persuasion through claims of having authority, credibility, and/or perceived expertise as validation for support and acceptance.
Pressure	Persuasion by using demands, persistence, or threats that may be overt or passive.

(Yukl, 1989)

For an individual in a leadership or managerial role, having the ability to influence followers or group members is essential to achieving goals and realizing a shared purpose and vision. Every member needs to be on board with the leader in order to move forward. Moreover, sometimes a leader will have a fully committed group but a necessary change requires the group to refocus and adjust to a new set of tasks or roles, and are asked to support a new or modified vision and purpose. A leader's ability to influence in a positive and compelling manner will impact their followers' continued commitment.

While some influence approaches may be second nature to some leaders or easily demonstrated, they often take time, experience, and practice to fully develop. Influence should come from a place of authenticity and transparency in order to be credible and meaningful for a leader's followers to accept. Forced or faked influence behaviors will not likely be successful, and a leader or manager should select the approaches they feel most comfortable with and competent in applying with ease given the composition of the group, and situational/contextual factors that may also impact the outcome. Another approach that leaders and managers may integrate with one or more influence tactics to give followers a greater sense of investment in and support for the leader and the group is empowerment, which we will discuss in the next section.

5.4 Effective Leadership Using Empowerment

While some leaders and managers believe that their followers or group members should hold little or no power because they could potentially undermine or challenge's their power, the most successful leaders with productive and engaged followers understand the value in sharing their power. In fact, a leader's own power and influence are typically reinforced when they share a reasonable degree of power, influence, and input with their followers or group members. This practice is referred to as empowerment. Empowerment of others is impactful because it can establish and sustain trust as well as perception of self-efficacy/competence, perceived value of individual contribution, and confidence. Consider a situation in which a teacher, manager, or person in charge enabled you to set your own goals, figure out how to perform certain tasks, and/or requested your input on a key decision or issue that needed a solution. More than likely, that leader's practice of empowering you resulted in a greater level of trust, the feeling of being a valued and important contributor to the group, and perhaps an enhanced level of self-confidence and feeling that the leader believes in your abilities to succeed without being micromanaged. These are some of the benefits that a leader or manager may derive from empowering their followers, team members, or staff.

The leadership practice of empowerment typically depends on various situational and contextual factors that will facilitate group member input and autonomy while also sustaining desired productivity, pragmatic decision making and other forms of member contribution, and timely goal attainment. Such factors may include the type and scope of the leader's role, organizational structure, operations and workflow (including the level of any associated risk), the group's composition and their knowledge, skills, and abilities (KSA's), and organizational norms and culture. Empowerment may be offered to group members through different opportunities that are relevant in their own respective roles as well as in their collaborative effort with the group, including the following behaviors and actions:

- Taking initiative on the selection of roles/assignments.

- Setting goals and timelines.

- Determining a suitable process or method for task completion.

- Communicating progress towards goals and performance to key stakeholders.

- Collaborating on a long-term strategic plan.

- Offering input in the evaluation of programs, processes, systems, products, or services.

- Sharing ideas as well as respectful, objective feedback on others' ideas.

- Assisting in the decision making process.

- Having access to necessary information.

- Making decisions regarding resource allocation.

Empowerment may increase engagement level and commitment because followers or group members are actively participating on a level of enhanced responsibility and control, which in turn will increase the perception of inclusion and investment. That said, it is important for a leader to consider a fair and equitable empowerment strategy among their followers, for a couple of reasons. If a follower observes other members being empowered by the leader while they are not, a decrease in engagement and performance could ensue and result in a situation similar to the out-group as described in the leader-member exchange (LMX) theory previously examined. Empowering all followers or members in a reasonably equitable manner will likely result in the collective empowerment of the group which may facilitate a trusting, participative, and highly engaged climate. This outcome would be similar to a leader having all of their followers within an LMX theory in-group context, with all members performing to their fullest potential, highly invested, cohesive, and supportive of one another through highs and lows.

While an empowered group may be fully capable and productive with minimal leader influence and intervention, the leader or manager should still continue to check in, assess the current status or situation, determine if anyone needs guidance, resources, or the leader's level of power and authority to 'step in' and handle an issue. Even though a follower, group member, or employee may really enjoy a certain degree of empowerment in their respective role, they often do still want the security and stability of having their leader in charge and responsible for the group in the event of crisis or high-risk, escalated situations. A leader should also clearly articulate the parameters of power among their followers to ensure realistic expectations and logical, pragmatic boundaries. For example, it would not typically be appropriate for a manager to allow their staff members to determine their rate of pay, job title, working conditions, essential duties, and the number of hours worked each week. In an organizational context, any structural components that are inherent and necessary for one's role should not be areas in which employees are empowered to adjust or modify (Dubrin, 2007). The awareness of when to give space and when to intervene is essential for a leader to understand and respect to sustain an impactful and supportive relationship with their group while also maintaining responsibility for the group and its performance outcomes and expected results.

While power and influence are separate concepts, it is clear that they are not only multifaceted and complex components of leadership but also strongly interconnected. Moreover, power and influence are directly aligned with a leader's unique personal attributes, their leadership style, and respective role. The most impactful leaders understand the responsibility and ethical requirements of holding such control, authority, and influential ability in their relationships with followers or group members and integrate their power and influence respectfully, fairly, and supportively into their leadership style. Leaders who exercise their power and influence effectively are able to have healthy and productive relationships with their followers, and at the same time drive consistently exemplary performance outcomes and results as they navigate their group towards their shared vision and purpose.

Chapter Summary

◆ Power refers to the potential or capacity to exert control over the behaviors, beliefs, and attitudes of others to achieve desired outcomes and results.

◆ The two main categories of power are personal power and position power. Personal power is comprised of expert, information, and referent power. Position power is comprised of legitimate, reward, and coercive power.

◆ There are four common outcomes of power: compliance, identification, internalization, and resistance.

◆ Influence refers to the use of behaviors and tactics offering sufficient control and persuasive ability to affect the responses of others and convince them to adopt a certain belief or act in a desired way.

◆ Empowerment refers to a leader's practice of sharing a reasonable degree of power, influence, and input with their followers, dependent on existing situational and contextual factors, often resulting in increased follower engagement and commitment to shared vision and goals.

Quiz 5

1. Of the four possible outcomes of power and influence, _____ refers to when the follower does what is asked but does not want to.

   a. compliance

   b. internalization

   c. identification

   d. resistance

2. Of the four possible outcomes of power and influence, _____ refers to when the follower does what is asked because the follower believes it is the right thing to do.

   a. compliance

   b. internalization

   c. identification

   d. resistance

3. A leader that has control over a group in a situation based on their formal role involving an assigned scope of authority over their group members most likely holds which type of power?

   a. Legitimate

   b. Information

   c. Persuasive

   d. Process

4. An individual with the ability to influence others through specialized knowledge, skills, or abilities most likely possesses _____ power.

    a. Prestige

    b. Expert

    c. Referent

    d. Coercive

5. A leader who is effective in garnering support from their followers through the logical and persuasive integration of factual information and evidence in their position is most likely using which influence tactic?

    a. Ingratiation

    b. Coalition

    c. Rational Persuasion

    d. Inspirational Appeals

Solutions to the above questions can be downloaded from
the **Online Resources** *section of this book on*
www.vibrantpublishers.com

Chapter **6**

Charismatic and Transformational Leadership

Now that we have a solid understanding of leadership in a broad context and a foundation of knowledge of the attributes, traits, and behaviors of effective leaders, including the critical role of power and influence, we can examine two leadership styles relevant and applicable to today's leaders in all areas of society.

In this chapter, our focus is on charismatic and transformational leadership. We will explore the distinctive facets of charisma and how leaders can leverage these unique and impactful attributes to appeal to followers to support their vision and mission, support and empower followers to contribute to goals and objectives in a manner that promotes engagement and commitment, and establish a trusted bond built on shared beliefs, values, and a collective purpose.

After reading this chapter, key learning objectives attained will include:

- Defining the elements that comprise charismatic and transformational leadership.

- Explaining the similarities and differences between charismatic and transformational leadership.

- Analyzing the individual and contextual factors that may contribute to a charismatic leader having a self-serving and/or negative vision, or a positive and morally sound vision that is beneficial to others.

- Applying the attributes and behaviors of charismatic and transformational leaders to the development and sustaining of real-world organizational best practices.

6.1 Charismatic Leadership

Why are some leaders more compelling and appealing than others, even when they possess similar knowledge, skills, and abilities? How are certain individuals able to draw people into their vision and ideas in a very profound and inspirational way, resulting in followers with unwavering loyalty and willingness to serve the leader's mission and directives? Some call this the 'x factor', that unique and special persona that makes certain leaders incredibly attractive and engaging to an audience that is highly motivated to be a part of their group. This unique persona is referred to as charisma. Charismatic people can be found in all parts of society and everyday life, but they are particularly important as leaders.

First, let's define charisma to better understand all of its facets and its role among the most influential leaders throughout history. The term charisma refers to a personal quality in an individual or leader composed of a combination of personality traits and behaviors that creates a compelling appeal for their followers, in turn, support their vision and goals because of their deep admiration towards the leader. Although many charismatic leaders do hold a direct leadership role with formal followers through position and reporting relationship (e.g., business, government, religious organizations, military), they can have followers through different channels (e.g., celebrities, sports heroes, entrepreneurs, innovators, social figures) in which a formal reporting relationship does not necessarily exist. The relationship between the charismatic leader and their followers is strong. Followers perceive charismatic leaders to be trustworthy, credible, powerful, dynamic, and passionate, and they would carry out any request for them.

Charismatic leaders can be found throughout history in all areas of society, such as the examples of well-known charismatic leaders in Table 6.1. Although their leadership has been impactful in different areas of society, they all have a set of attributes, personality characteristics, and behaviors in common that depict charisma. In the next section, we will examine in-depth the attributes and personal characteristics typically embodied by charismatic leaders.

Table 6.1

Government & Military	Religion	Social Justice & Civil Rights	Business and Organizations
Former U.S. President Franklin Delano Roosevelt (FDR)	Mohandas Gandhi	Dr. Martin Luther King, Jr.	Virgin CEO Sir Richard Branson
Former U.S. President John F. Kennedy (JFK)	Saint (Mother) Teresa of Calcutta	Nelson Mandela	Tesla CEO Elon Musk
Former British Prime Minister Sir Winston Churchill	The Dalai Lama	Princess Diana of Wales	Former GE CEO Jack Welch

6.2 Attributes and Characteristics of Charismatic Leaders

Charismatic leaders often demonstrate similar types of attributes, personality traits, and behaviors, even in different environments or situations. While many successful and respected leaders typically have one or more of these elements, charismatic leaders will possess most (sometimes all) of these elements.

Visionary

- Vision and mission are viewed as noble, important, symbolic, innovative, and cutting-edge.

- Vision goes beyond the mundane and status quo, but not perceived as too radical or outside what is considered reasonable parameters.

- Charismatic leaders have the ability to see long-term potential and opportunities and how to achieve goals designed to make significant and positive long-range impact (i.e., a better way).

Dynamic

- Charismatic leaders are passionate about their beliefs and values and emotionally expressive about their vision and purpose, with high energy, enthusiasm, and achievement-orientation.

- Charismatic leaders demonstrate dramatic, sometimes risky and fearless behaviors.

- Charismatic leaders have magnetic personalities and are strongly appealing to their followers, with an assertive confidence and sometimes unconventional style.

Inspirational

- Charismatic leaders have masterful communication skills and are highly persuasive.

- Charismatic leaders inspire trust through their rapport and strong bond with their followers.

- Charismatic leaders enable followers' self-efficacy – the belief that they can accomplish lofty goals and reach their fullest potential – so that the leader's high expectations can be met.

- Charismatic leaders make followers feel proud and capable by offering praise and recognition, enhancing follower support and investment in the shared vision and mission.

In addition to these common elements, many charismatic leaders will demonstrate complementary attributes that have a profound effect on their followers, such as impressive breadth and/or depth of expertise in a particular area, multiple types of power (e.g., referent, legitimate), and a level of perceived competence that appears to be above and beyond the norm. In the next section, we will examine the effect of the unique bond between a charismatic leader and their followers.

6.3 Charismatic Leadership Impact on Followers

A charismatic leader is able to effectively leverage their attributes and appeal to develop and cultivate a trusting and loyal bond with their followers. This bond is essential for the leader to rely on their willingness to support the mission and goals enthusiastically and often without question. To achieve this bond, a charismatic leader will persuasively and competently describe their vision to enable others to see its value and conceptualize how they may play an important role in its attainment, even if the vision is novel, unusual, or out of the norm.

In many situations, a charismatic leader is particularly impactful when followers are dissatisfied with some circumstance or event and seek change to what is perceived as broken, unfair, inadequate, or antiquated. The leader arrives, points out the inadequacies of what currently exists, obtains agreement and support from the group on the need for change, and offers their vision for a new or better way. Follower support and enthusiasm are even greater when they are under some type of stress or duress that they believe the leader can remove and create a better outcome.

Research conducted by House (1977) provides key insights among a charismatic leader's followers, including these common themes among followers in different groups and settings led by charismatic leaders:

- Followers hold a high level of trust in the correctness of the leader's beliefs.

- Followers unquestioningly accept the leader's position of dominance.

- Followers are completely willing to obey the leader.

- Followers share similar beliefs to those of the leader.

- Followers have a strong emotional connection to the leader.

- Followers identify with and admire the leader.

- Followers have a strong connection/involvement with the leader's mission.

- Followers accept the leader's high level of performance expectations.

- Followers believe their contribution will impact the mission being accomplished.

The relationship between a charismatic leader and their followers is typically a mutually beneficial, respected, and trusted partnership. In exchange for follower loyalty and willingness to contribute to the collective goals and mission with full commitment and involvement, the charismatic leader gives their followers a sense of identity, purpose, belonging, and meaning as well as emotional support, confidence, and encouragement. As this partnership evolves and matures, the vision and mission become fully internalized by the followers and the level of cohesion and dedication are strong and unwavering. When the charismatic leader is a decent and worthy role model and sets an example of integrity and morals, the outcomes are typically positive for everyone; however; not all charismatic leaders use their appeal and persuasion for noble causes, and there are examples of charismatic leaders whose narcissism and destructive focus wreaked havoc and destroyed lives. In the next section, we will examine the negative side of charismatic leadership.

6.4 The Negative Side of Charismatic Leadership

A charismatic leader can have a negative agenda, yet still attract loyal followers willing to carry out their directives and mission even if the outcomes are harmful or destructive. This is the power of charisma. Moreover, a charismatic leader can still be highly effective even though their vision is destructive and will result in tragic outcomes for many individuals. Consider some examples of negative, self-serving charismatic leaders throughout history that wielded control over many die hard followers, often in roles such as dictators and other government leaders, business leaders, and cult leaders: Adolph Hitler, Fidel Castro, Charles Manson, David Koresh, and Kenneth Lay and Jeffrey Skilling (the executives that caused the collapse of Enron). A negative charismatic leader can start off with a lofty vision that may not be initially perceived as radical or destructive, but once loyal followers are in place the leader can adjust the goals, decisions, and actions towards the more extreme desired plan that serves their actual dangerous and destructive vision.

While positive and negative charismatic leaders share some common attributes, those leaders with a destructive or dangerous agenda will also typically exhibit narcissism, extremes in emotional state and mood, unpredictability, impulsivity, and aggressiveness. As a result, they can overestimate themselves and their own importance, believing that they are above the law, moral codes of ethics and conduct, and the guidelines and regulations of any other individual or entity. Destructive charismatic leaders are often oppressive with their followers, and will keep them dependent and loyal to the leader. They may be unwilling to conduct succession planning and allow others to prepare for or promote into a leadership role. They prefer to keep their followers in a subordinate position and dependent on them. Negative charismatic leaders may also have extremely high expectations and requirements for their compliance, with little in return. The followers lower their expectations and needs, being satisfied with very little in return from the leader. The leader's focus is on their own self-serving goals and personal agenda, even at the cost of negative or harmful consequences to their followers and the greater population.

A useful approach to determine whether a charismatic leader has a positive or negative focus and agenda is to consider the potential outcomes for their followers and other individuals or groups that are impacted by the leader's mission and actions. If followers and others are largely impacted in a positive, healthy, and productive manner, then most likely the leader is using their charisma for a good and moral purpose. If the opposite holds true in which the leader's followers and others are impacted in a harmful, destructive, or toxic manner, then the leader is most likely a negative charismatic leader (Yukl, 1998). Those charismatic leaders whose vision and purpose are worthy, ethical, and beneficial to others may also be considered transformational in nature which we will review in the next section.

6.5 Transformational Leadership

Transformational leadership can be found in all types of organizations, institutions, and environments throughout society. Transformational leaders also possess charismatic attributes but unlike purely charismatic leaders, they do not leverage these attributes for a personal agenda or self-serving interests. They strive to raise awareness and produce outcomes that positively impact as many individuals and groups as possible. Some well-known leaders noted in our previous section are considered transformational and charismatic leaders, including Dr. Martin Luther King, Jr., and Saint (Mother) Teresa of Calcutta. The transformational leader helps bring about major, positive changes that go beyond their own self-interests to meet the needs of a larger group or population. They serve as a social architect, creating purpose and objectives around the need for change, something that others can resonate with and support.

From the perspective of personality traits and characteristics, transformational leaders also demonstrate the visionary, dynamic, and inspirational behaviors previously discussed. Transformational leaders often demonstrate a high level of emotional intelligence, with a greater capability for empathy, compassion, and diplomacy, and focus on developing and sustaining mutually beneficial relationships with others than purely charismatic leaders typically exhibit. Researchers (Bass, 1985; Avolio, 1999) have provided insightful findings on core transformational leader behaviors, often referred to as the 'Four I's' and depicted in Table 6.2, believed to be intrinsic to transformational leaders.

Table 6.2

Idealized Influence	Inspirational Motivation	Intellectual Stimulation	Individual Consideration
Demonstrate charismatic personality traits	Generates passion and drive in followers, creating engagement	Provides challenging yet attainable goals	Listens to followers' needs and concerns
Appeal and admiration	Has high expectations of followers	Ensures work is interesting and meaningful	Provides clear, specific direction and the tools and resources needed to perform tasks
Serves as a positive role model	Encourages followers to achieve	Encourages creativity and innovative ideas	Offers guidance and coaching
Demonstrates optimism and enthusiasm	Shares meaningful, and emotionally-driven appeals that inspire followers	Supports prudent risk taking and disciplined thinking	Invests in and takes care of followers
			Shows gratitude and celebrates successes together

(Bass, 1985; Avolio, 1999)

In addition to these personal attributes, transformational leaders will understand the concept of transactional leadership and know how to leverage this style to enable their followers and group members to provide sustained strong performance and achievement-orientation. Transactional leadership focuses on the exchange that will benefit all the parties involved, so there is a clear benefit to each individual follower or group member for their contribution and performance, as well as the benefit to the collective group and the larger population they serve.

The expectation is that followers or group members will be accountable for completing tasks, meeting performance outcomes, and attaining goals determined by the leader in exchange for a positive outcome such as a reward or recognition, continued investment in their personal development and growth, or other relevant benefit. Sometimes a transactional leader will facilitate opportunities for followers to achieve success through 'easy wins' at first and then graduate to more complex tasks, expectations, and goals. Once this exchange is met and satisfactory to everyone, the bigger picture of achieving a positive change that will benefit the greater population can be accomplished. This win-win-win approach offers more realistically sustainable performance from everyone, rather than relying on the idea that individuals will stay properly motivated for the greater good without any sense of personal outcomes.

Whereas transactional and charismatic leadership styles can exist on their own, transformational leaders have the ability to seamlessly weave the best of both styles into their own unique style to benefit themselves (to some extent), their followers, and the external community or larger external population. Bass (1985) proposed that a transformational leader will integrate aspects of transactional leadership in their approach with followers or group members. In an organizational context, transformational leadership has demonstrated significantly better employee job satisfaction, motivation, group/organizational performance, and perceived leader performance as compared to other leadership styles such as pure charismatic, transactional, and laissez-faire which is a style that exhibits minimal to no leader presence, direction, or influence on followers (Howell & Avolio, 1998; Judge & Piccolo, 2004).

The transformational leader will demonstrate a purposeful balance of the appropriate charismatic and transactional behaviors that will inspire and support their followers so that together, they drive necessary change. Transformational leaders build a following of supporters through their charismatic style and together they motivate and elevate one another to higher levels of morality and service to others to usher in positive changes and improvements that benefit the greater good (Burns, 1978). Transformational leaders have a strong and positive influence on their followers. There is a synergetic and loyal partnership between the transformational leader and their followers, which creates a climate of shared values, empowerment, and responsibility for contributing to a vision and mission that everyone understands will have a profound and far-reaching effect on a larger external population.

As we conclude our exploration of charismatic and transformational leadership, it is important to remember that both styles are valuable and have great potential to facilitate meaningful and beneficial outcomes to a larger community or population. They have the capability to appeal to followers that will support their vision, perceive their efforts and contributions as an expression of themselves, and share their strengths and talents to serve the mission of the group. Charismatic and transformational leaders both have the capacity to create a community built upon trust, mutual respect, transparency, empathy, and shared values so that everyone in invested is working together as a catalyst for change.

Chapter Summary

◆ A charismatic leader embodies a unique combination of personality traits and demonstrates behaviors that create a compelling appeal for their followers, who in turn support their vision and goals because of their deep admiration towards the leader.

◆ The relationship between a charismatic leader and their followers is supported by a strong and trusted bond. Followers often perceive a charismatic leader to be a visionary, credible, powerful, dynamic, and inspirational, and are willing to carry out any requests for them.

◆ While many charismatic leaders have a positive and rational vision, some can have a self-serving or negative vision and attract loyal followers willing to carry out their directives and mission due to their powerful charism and persuasive ability.

◆ While positive and negative charismatic leaders share some common attributes, those leaders with a destructive or dangerous agenda may also exhibit narcissism, extremes in emotional state and mood, unpredictability, impulsivity, and aggressiveness.

◆ Transformational leaders also possess charismatic attributes but they do not leverage these attributes solely for a personal agenda or self-serving interests. Rather, they strive to raise awareness and produce positive outcomes for as many individuals and groups as possible.

◆ Transformational leaders and their followers also have a strong and loyal partnership, supported by a climate of shared values, empowerment, and responsibility for contributing to a vision and mission that everyone understands will have a profound and beneficial effect on a larger population.

Quiz 6

1. **A manager who gives new employees easy assignments that they are almost certain to complete successfully and then praises them for their success is most likely demonstrating which of the following characteristics of charismatic leadership?**

    a. Masterful communication skills

    b. Ability to inspire trust

    c. Ability to make group members feel capable

    d. Energy and action orientation

2. **Which of the following can be an issue and concern with some charismatic leaders?**

    a. Their vision is not always clear and compelling to their followers

    b. They can have difficulty in effectively influencing others through lack of persuasion

    c. They can sometimes lead followers down an unethical, self-serving path

    d. They place unreasonable, unrealistically high expectations on group members

3. **A leader that expects followers to complete delegated tasks and achieve set goals in exchange for a positive and desired outcome or benefit is likely demonstrating which leadership style?**

   a. Transformational

   b. Transactional

   c. Charismatic

   d. Transitional

4. **A transformational leader is one who** _____.

   a. transforms their leadership style to fit the situation

   b. makes major changes in an organization to benefit a small, select group

   c. desires to move up the corporate ladder rapidly

   d. partners with their followers to drive change that benefits the greater good

5. A transformational leader who provides challenging yet attainable goals is likely demonstrating which of the following elements referred to as the 'Four I's'?

   a. Intellectual Stimulation

   b. Inspirational Motivation

   c. Idealized Influence

   d. Individual Consideration

Solutions to the above questions can be downloaded from
the **Online Resources** *section of this book on*
www.vibrantpublishers.com

Chapter 7

Leading High Performance Teams

Most – if not all – of us have been part of a team at some point, whether it was a socially-based team, a sports team, an academic/class team, or a professional work-based team. A team enables a group of individuals to work together to achieve a common goal or purpose in which members rely on each other's contributions to attain an outcome that benefits everyone. Each team member offers unique and valuable input which integrates like pieces of a puzzle. Effective team members are active contributors to a common purpose, have specific roles aligned with their knowledge and skills, perform tasks and responsibilities relevant to clear goals, and share in the accountability of the team's collective performance and outcomes. From an organizational perspective, teams have evolved in recent years from forming occasionally to a more widespread and strategic component of organizational operations. In many situations, a team leader is an appropriate role to coordinate team members, tasks, and logistics to ensure team goals are achieved, processes run smoothly, and team member relations are positive and supportive.

In this chapter, we will apply many of the concepts and practices covered in the previous chapters to strategic team leadership and examine the best practices that support and sustain high performance teams.

After reading this chapter, key learning objectives attained will include:

- Understanding organizational shifts over time that have resulted in the increasing need for teams.

- Describing different types of team leaders, and how leadership behaviors may be contributed by team members without any type of leader role in place.

- Applying task-focused and interpersonal relationship-focused behaviors as an effective approach to leading high performance teams.

- Analyzing the elements of team leadership that result in team success and achievement of collective performance outcomes and objectives.

7.1 The Evolution of Teams in Organizations

Several factors have influenced the increase in the deployment of organizational teams in recent years, including shifts in the nature of the work itself, changes to the traditional organizational structure, and the rise of technology and globalization.

These factors do not exist on their own in a vacuum, but are interconnected. Every type of organization has been impacted by one or more of these factors in some manner, resulting in an increased reliance on collaboration through teamwork.

As work complexity continues to increase, it has become less feasible and efficient in many situations for individuals to complete various multifaceted tasks and types of work without the input of others. It is also becoming less common for one person to see a typical project from start to finish. A collective effort from multiple individuals with different but complementary knowledge, skills, and experience is often needed to meet increasingly complex needs. Organizations have responded by developing and sustaining high performing teams with cross-functional competencies and the agility to collaborate and make key decisions together.

In terms of structure, organizations have been evaluating the more traditional elements of their composition and redesigning a new, flatter structure, with fewer layers and hierarchical reporting relationships. That said, the responsibilities of supervisors and managers that once comprised those layers continue to exist. Strategic planning is still a necessary organizational process, as well as the coordination of complex operations and systems and decision making. Someone still needs to address these critical organizational needs, resulting in the strategic implementation of teams to serve this purpose. Moreover, the nature of work today can no longer accommodate lengthy approval processes or waiting for signatures from multiple levels of management before making a decision or moving forward on a particular action. A team effort where each member contributes to a team decision or plan of action is typically more time efficient in today's more streamlined organizations.

With a continued increase in globalization, many individual contributors no longer share geographic proximity with their co-workers which has resulted in the need for virtual teams, collaborating through an array of technology systems and tools designed for remote communication, electronic workflow processes, and knowledge/document sharing. Additionally, the evolution of highly sophisticated technology tools and systems has enabled organizational operations and processes to occur with greater speed and responsiveness which have become a business imperative. Organizations must be positioned to swiftly respond to demands from global customers and other stakeholders in a manner that may not be realistic for one person to satisfactorily accomplish. In many circumstances, a collective effort is necessary to quickly pivot, re-focus, and deliver on changing needs and expectations.

With a cohesive and focused team in place, problems and issues can be analyzed collectively by team members contributing unique and valuable knowledge, skills, and abilities (KSA's), innovative ideas and solutions can be generated from diverse team member experiences and perspectives, and quality decisions can be made based on a collaborative effort (Parker, 1990). Organizational teams may be structured in different ways depending on their purpose and composition and are referred to using an array of terms, such as cross-functional teams, task forces, project teams, and committees. They can have a specified end date once a goal or objective is reached (e.g., a systems implementation task force) or continue indefinitely to serve an ongoing need (e.g., a safety committee). As focus and investment in organizational teams continues to increase, team leadership will be critically important to facilitate team effectiveness. In the next section, we will examine common approaches to team leadership.

7.2 Types of Team Leadership

Regardless of a team's purpose or structure, leadership behaviors and actions are essential to facilitating team effort, cohesion, performance, and results. Rarely does a team achieve all of its goals and objectives without anyone on the team contributing some degree of leadership or direction at some point along the way. Team leadership processes, however they are applied, should be in place to facilitate the performance outcomes needed to achieve desired results through the collective effort of team member contributions (Zaccaro, Rittman, & Marks, 2001). Team leadership may be formal or informal, shared among team members as a collective responsibility, or assigned to one person at a time as either a permanent or rotating role. Figure 7.1 highlights two common team leadership approaches: a self-managed, more informal type of team leadership, and a more formal, structured team leadership.

7.2.1 Self-managed/Informal Team Leadership

Sometimes referred to as a 'leaderless' team, a team that is self-managed and does not have an official team leader role can and should still integrate leadership behaviors and processes. With informal team leadership, any team member can contribute leadership behaviors at any time, often occurring organically based on the needs of the situation and the attributes and KSA's of the team member best suited to offer their input. Team members are empowered to contribute relevant leadership behaviors as needed. In order for this approach to work effectively, team members do need to be highly cohesive and have a strong interpersonal bond for members to respect the direction of a peer member and be willing to follow their lead, and also be confident enough to step up and lead should a need arise that is aligned with their own strengths. A set of team norms and expectations composed of clear boundaries and parameters is essential for members of a team relying on an informal, leaderless structure to understand the limitations of any one member's control and input. With these elements in place, the team will usually support the leadership behaviors that members contribute at different times because they understand the importance of having leadership direction in various areas based on expertise, which in turn will facilitate success for everyone.

7.2.2 Formal Team Leadership

With formal team leadership, a structured team leader role is typically assigned to one member responsible for managing the team's tasks, interpersonal functions, and performance. This leadership role can be indefinite, for a specified period of time, or shared among members and rotated on a regular schedule. The team leader role can also be strategically delegated based on the phases of a goal being accomplished (Levi, 2017). For example, a project team responsible for the implementation of a new technology system may have to work through several project phases: budgetary approval, system selection and implementation, and communication and training for the workforce. While in the first project phase, an appropriate team leader may be a member with KSA's from the finance function. The second phase may be more effectively led by a member from IT, and the last phase may be best managed by a team member from the human resources or training function. Each team leader will have milestone tasks and responsibilities relevant to their organizational role and function-specific skills and competencies while leading during their respective project phase. Even though this team leadership approach is role-driven and structured, it can be designed in creative ways depending on the team's unique purpose, composition, and goals.

Figure 7.1

Self-managed/Informal	**Structured Role/Formal**
No official leader role; leadership behaviors emerge organically from members based on needed KSA's and expertise, and are respected, accepted and supported by the team	A structured, assigned team leader role exists; a member may assume role based on their KSA's and team needs for a period of time; role may be shared or rotated

Whether informal or formal team leadership is in place, a collaborative and engaged team will still need an effective combination of task and relationship focused behaviors to ensure they maintain trust, communication, cooperation, and productivity. In the next section, we will revisit these behavioral approaches in the context of team leadership.

7.3 Balancing Task Focus and Interpersonal Team Needs

Just as a traditional leader should demonstrate a relevant balance of task-focused and interpersonal relationship-focused behaviors with their followers or group members, a team leader also needs to integrate both types of behaviors and actions in their approach with team members. The most appropriate balance of task and relationship-oriented behaviors will still depend on the team's objectives, day-to-day operations and performance expectations, and different situational factors that may arise, such as a deadline or schedule change or a conflict among team members. Table 7.1 highlights essential team leadership behaviors and actions that facilitate task focus as well as interpersonal relationship needs and team cohesion.

Table 7.1

Task Facilitation	Interpersonal Relationship Facilitation
Sets collective team goals and individual member goals, and clarifies performance expectations	Encourages an environment of mutual respect, inclusion, and trust
Determines team roles and assigns to members; ensures role clarity and commitment	Establishes behavioral expectations and norms by setting up ground rules or a team charter
Develops work schedules and deadlines; delegates tasks to appropriate team members	Creates a culture of socialization, support, and interdependence so members can identify with the team mission and how to work together cohesively
Provides direction and instructions for completing tasks, including necessary resources	Diffuses negative emotions and behaviors; manages and resolves conflict among members
Coordinates team meetings including logistics and agenda; holds members accountable for delivering on action items	Encourages input and contributions from everyone to share ideas and perspectives
Checks in with team members regularly on work status and task completion, ensuring all needs are met and resources are accessible	Offers recognition and appreciation to team members, both individually and collectively, for their efforts and achievements
Evaluates processes to consider what works or doesn't work, needed modifications, and issues that need to be addressed and resolved	Encourage team pride by emphasizing the importance of their purpose and excellence in their collaborative effort and accomplishments

(Larson & LaFasto, 1989; Hackman, 2012)

A team leader will undoubtedly experience highs and lows, successes and challenges with their team along the way. Even the most effective and high-performing team will have conflicts, productivity plateaus, and obstacles to overcome. Being an effective team leader does not mean micromanaging or acting like a "boss" or authority figure, but rather as a navigator and facilitator of sustainable team member engagement, support, and results-oriented performance. Our last section of this chapter will explore an array of success factors that a team leader can integrate into their own unique approach.

7.4 Team Leadership Success Factors

Though different teams and circumstances will have unique and diverse needs, there is a set of best practices that can be broadly applied for leading with impact. An important element for any team leader is the ability to balance a dual role as a team leader and team player/contributor. Team members must perceive the leader to be in a position with some degree of control and willing to accept directives from this individual, but also acknowledge the leader will jump into team tasks and activities as a collaborator. Members should respect when the leader role needs to take precedence. Without this element, the team leader will likely have difficulty attaining goals and desired outcomes.

A successful team leader should be a strategic thinker, always considering short and long-term goals in determining team direction and focus. With a clear and meaningful purpose in place, a team leader should ensure all members understand and support the team mission and plan for objectives to accomplish. They will also need to maintain awareness of the bigger picture and make sure the team's internal processes are aligned with organizational needs and changes outside the scope of the team (Zaccaro et al., 2001). Strong networking skills and the ability to build alliances and relationships with other team leaders and key external stakeholders are also important. These relationships will enable the team leader to act on behalf of the team as a liaison and representative to obtain support on plans and decisions from stakeholders, secure resources, to facilitate recognition and rewards, and to gather important external information and updates to report back to the team. The team should feel confident that their team leader is serving as their advocate and keeping them updated by sharing information and resources through ongoing communication. In terms of strategic evaluation of team performance, a leader should measure productivity and outcomes using metrics that assess results through key performance indicators (KPI's).

Lastly, a team leader should show empathy to demonstrate that they can see the needs, challenges, and interests of team members through their lens and perspective. Team members will be more invested and willing to contribute if they perceive the leader understands their role and responsibility to the team and is not asking or expecting them to contribute in ways they are not ready to contribute themselves. They are responsive to each team member's unique 'WIIFM' (What's In It For Me) needs in a way that highlights the individual benefits and outcomes that come with active participation. The team leader is available to listen to concerns, answer questions, and offer clarification to ensure their 'ask' of each team member is clear, fair, appropriate to their role, and in balance with what is being asked of everyone else. (Dubrin, 2007). Additionally, an empathetic team leader will explain how the performance outcomes of individual members integrate together to produce collective results which encourages a greater sense of commitment and interdependence among team members (i.e., no one team member can reach the goals by themselves).

With any type of team structure and purpose, there will be some semblance of leadership behaviors in place even though how they are employed and by whom may differ depending on the nature of the team and its context. That said, teams will always require that members share the responsibility for supporting mutual respect and trust, open communication, conscientiousness and dependability, engagement, cooperation, and the professionalism to self-manage as a collective entity. These responsibilities are essential for everyone to stay focused and in alignment with the team's purpose and objectives. Leadership behaviors will be a necessary element to sustain this great responsibility and to ensure the team's performance and outcomes effectively contribute to an organization's vision and mission.

Chapter Summary

◆ Teams are a common occurrence in many areas of society, and have continued to increase in number among all types of organizations as a result of influencing factors such as shifts in the nature of work and performance output, changes to the traditional organizational structure, and the rise of technology and globalization.

◆ Team leadership may be structured based on team's purpose, goals, and composition, and may be formal or informal, shared among team members as a collective responsibility, or assigned to one person at a time as either a permanent or rotating role.

◆ Team leaders should strive to implement the most appropriate balance of tasks and relationship-oriented approaches depending on the team's objectives, day-to-day operations and performance expectations, and situational/contextual factors that may arise.

◆ Though different teams will have unique and diverse needs, successful team leaders can be most impactful by demonstrating competence as a team leader and a team player/contributor by strategically planning and navigating short and long-term goals, by serving as a proactive liaison between the team and external stakeholders, and by supporting team members through a genuine showing of empathy and understanding of their needs, concerns, and interests.

◆ As focus and investment in organizational teams continues to increase, team leadership will be critically important to facilitate team effectiveness.

Quiz 7

1. All of the following trends have influenced the increase in the number of organizational teams with the exception of _____.

   a. an increase in artificial intelligence

   b. a shift towards a flatter organizational structure

   c. an increase in work complexity

   d. the availability of technology tools and systems

2. A team comprised of members that work in different organizational departments and contribute their respective field-specific knowledge and experience to support the team's objectives is often referred to as a _____ team.

   a. virtual

   b. self-managed

   c. cross-functional

   d. global

3. Which of the following characteristics is not consistent with a structured, formal team leader role?

   a. The team leader will receive a promotion for their efforts

   b. There is typically one assigned team leader at a time

   c. Any team member can be assigned the team leader role

   d. The team leader role can be rotated on a time schedule

4. **Which is the following is not an example of a task facilitation behavior?**

    a. Sets clear and tangible goals

    b. Coordinates team meetings

    c. Diffuses conflict among team members

    d. Checks in with team members on task progress

5. **A team leader's ability to show their understanding and respect for team members' perceptions of their situation, needs, and challenges is referred to as _____.**

    a. empathy

    b. validation

    c. consideration

    d. sympathy

Solutions to the above questions can be downloaded from
the **Online Resources** *section of this book on*
www.vibrantpublishers.com

Chapter 8

Leadership Development

All organizations must strive to acquire, develop, and retain the most talented, capable workforce they can to achieve their goals and objectives, and sustain growth, agility, and responsiveness to changing global conditions and trends. Investment in a learning and development strategy is essential for meeting this need, for individuals at all levels within the organization. Leaders and managers have their own unique needs for acquiring the knowledge, skills, and abilities (KSA's) required for their current roles as well as preparing them for long-term projected role shifts. Throughout this book, we have examined the attributes, KSA's, and associated behaviors of effective leaders; however, effective leadership does not typically just happen naturally and will require some level of support through training and learning opportunities.

The focus of this chapter is on leadership development and coaching strategies including an assessment of different approaches and their application in various settings, and the importance of the alignment between leadership development strategy and performance outcomes relevant to organizational goals.

After reading this chapter, key learning objectives attained will include:

- Understanding the purpose and value of leadership development within an organization.

- Defining the term competencies and describing the behavioral competencies essential for leader/manager effectiveness.

- Examining an array of leadership development methods and approaches and their appropriate implementation.

- Assessing key best practices that are essential to building and sustaining and effective, efficient leadership development strategy.

8.1 The Importance of Leadership Development

For organizations to deliver on their mission and purpose, they must have a competent workforce with the expertise, skills, and abilities to serve as the engine for performance outcomes that drive the organization forward. A learning and development strategy aligned with changing needs and goals is a business imperative for all functional areas and levels of the workforce, from early career staff and professionals to departmental and business unit managers and to senior leaders. A significant benefit of ongoing learning and development is the increased agility for organizations to seamlessly pivot and lean into shifting needs with minimal disruption or a lengthy learning curve because they have a flexible, highly-skilled (often cross-functional) workforce. Even senior leaders with years of experience still benefit immensely from regular development activities and programs. Leadership development is never a 'one and done' event but rather an ongoing process as new knowledge and skills must be acquired and honed in response to changing circumstances and expectations. Additionally, leadership development is important for long-range career planning for early-career and mid-level professionals to prepare themselves for future leadership roles, referred to as succession planning.

Succession planning is a strategic process for identifying and developing individuals to move into roles of progressively increasing responsibility and leadership/management scope. It would be short-sighted and ineffective for an organization to allow its senior leaders to leave their respective positions through retirement, promotion, or resignation without ensuring a transfer of their knowledge and intellectual capital to other internal staff for continuity and sustainability. While the focus of succession planning is typically more long-term and future-oriented, it is important to always have this strategy in place and not just when it is known that a leader will move on in the near future. Unpredictable events can always occur, such as an abrupt resignation, an incapacitating illness, or a leader's unexpected death. Careful planning is essential to ensure everyone has opportunities for development, whether or not they have expressed a desire for career growth. Sometimes, a person's long term goal is not known and it may take time to build one's professional road map, but that does not mean it is appropriate to focus only on the most career-minded and ambitious among the workforce. Another benefit of succession planning is brand

and culture retention because employees that grow their careers internally to assume leader roles will be more fully immersed and engaged in the organization's culture and branding compared to an external person hired directly into a leadership role.

This engagement factor is another advantage of building workforce talent and readiness for growth within the organization. Through learning and development, career planning, goal setting, and accessible opportunities for advancement, internal staff will more likely perceive that the organization values them and genuinely wants to invest in their professional development and goal achievement, which will enhance employee engagement, dedication, and commitment. The key for alignment of these elements is for leadership development to integrate with other workforce strategies including hiring and selection, performance management, and other learning and development initiatives. This is really the best method for understanding the existing level of KSA's of the current workforce, identifying any gaps or short/long-term needs, and associating those KSA's with the demonstrated behaviors expected in each type of position or role. These behaviors are also referred to as competencies, which we will examine in the next section.

8.2 Leadership Competencies

Prior to the design of leadership development programs, a thorough needs assessment should be conducted that examines the KSAs and behaviors required for effectively preparing individuals to lead and manage in different types of roles. To accomplish this needs assessment, a competency-based approach can be very helpful. Competencies are defined as "sets of behaviors that are instrumental in the delivery of desired results or outcomes" (Kurz and Bartram, 2002). Competencies focus on an individual's attributes, knowledge, and skills that will enable observable behaviors and actions to meet performance expectations and drive desired results. Competency models may be developed based on a functional area, leadership/management responsibility, and other niche contextual categories important to the role, or can be layered together. For example, the role of IT Manager would benefit from a combination of functional/technical competencies as well as leadership/managerial competencies. Even though the functional competencies may vary, the leadership/managerial competencies could apply broadly to anyone with that responsibility.

There are a variety of helpful resources and tools for developing competency models, though perhaps the most well-known and respected published competency model is the Lominger Standard Competencies, based on over 15 years of research by Lombardo and Eichinger (1998). These 67 competencies, as listed in Table 8.1, can be used in multiple combinations and customized to fit specific roles.

Table 8.1

The 67 Lominger Standard Competencies				
Action Oriented	Dealing With Ambiguity	Approach-ability	Boss Relationships	Business Acumen
Career Ambition	Caring About Direct Reports	Comfort Around Higher Management	Command Skills	Compassion
Composure	Conflict Management	Confronting Direct Reports	Creativity	Customer Focus
Timely Decision Making	Decision Quality	Delegation	Developing Direct Reports	Directing Others
Managing Diversity	Ethics and Values	Fairness to Direct Reports	Functional/ Technical Skills	Hiring and Staffing
Humor	Informing	Innovation Management	Integrity and Trust	Intellectual Horsepower
Interpersonal Savvy	Learning on the Fly	Listening	Managerial Courage	Managing and Measuring Work
Motivating Others	Negotiating	Organizational Agility	Organizing	Dealing With Paradox
Patience	Peer Relationships	Perseverance	Personal Disclosure	Personal Learning
Perspective	Planning	Political Savvy	Presentation Skills	Priority Setting
Problem Solving	Process Management	Drive For Results	Self-Development	Self-Knowledge
Sizing Up People	Standing Alone	Strategic Agility	Managing Through Systems	Building Effective Teams
Technical Learning	Time Management	Total Quality Management and Reengineering	Under-standing Others	Managing Vision and Purpose
Work/Life Balance	Written Communi-cations			

(Lombardo & Eichinger, 1998)

While these competencies could be relevant for all types of leaders and managers, certain competencies are more applicable to different types of leader roles and contexts. This is the benefit of implementing a competency-based approach to leadership development – there is no need to recreate a complete set of behaviors from scratch for every distinct role. Additionally, it is a more simple and effective approach to develop a competency model and use it as a benchmark for designing appropriate leadership development programs and initiatives, which will be examined in the next section.

8.3 Leadership Development Approaches

A leadership development strategy can integrate a variety of formal and informal approaches depending on needs and goals including degree and certificate-conferring educational programs, workshops and classes, mentoring programs, manager/executive coaching, experiential, and hands-on learning opportunities. Sometimes learning and development initiatives are designed as scheduled, structured events and at other times they are more unstructured, ad hoc activities integrated within day-to-day operations. A combination approach is common because the breadth and depth of the competencies previously discussed will typically be more effectively and efficiently developed through different methods. For example, managers developing themselves in the area of conflict resolution would benefit from a training class highlighting various conflict resolution techniques, but a more effective approach may be a combination of classroom instruction followed by hands-on practice through role play scenarios with a mentor or coach. The following sections highlight several effective leadership development approaches, including formal education programs, training classes and workshops, mentoring and coaching, and experiential, hands-on learning opportunities.

8.3.1 Formal Degree/Certificate Education Programs

There are many formal leadership educational opportunities offering degrees or certification upon successful completion. Degree programs typically provide a broad curriculum comprised of different functional areas (e.g., MBA), or a curriculum relevant to certain fields and disciplines (e.g., finance, healthcare management). Certificate programs are also an option for developing focused knowledge and skills in a niche area (e.g., Lean Six Sigma). These programs may be offered in-person or online, with the latter becoming an increasingly appealing and practical option for working professionals. Organizations may also offer funding and reimbursement for individuals enrolled in external leadership educational programs, which is a valuable benefit.

8.3.2 Training Classes and Workshops

Unlike degree and certification programs composed of a broader curriculum, standalone training workshops and classes can be customized to meet current and projected needs. They can be developed as in-person or online programs and in sessions ranging from a few hours to several days, depending on the breadth and depth of the content being covered and the programs goals or objectives. For example, a one-day workshop on conflict resolution for managers can be offered as needed and can be integrated into a more comprehensive training program for new managers along with other topics such as delegation skills and team building. With training courses built as distinct and separate programs, they can be offered by themselves or 'bundled' depending on the need and time frame.

8.3.3 Mentoring and Coaching

A mentoring program can be a valuable opportunity for an early to mid-career professional to have one-on-one dialogue and guidance from a senior member of the organization on a diverse mix of topics. A mentor can offer applied, real-world advice based on their own experiences, trial and error, and best practices adopted over the years, and be available to answer questions that arise for the mentee. Mentoring can occur informally when leaders and senior management meet and get to know junior members of the organization and naturally develop professional relationships. Informal mentoring can be just as beneficial as formal mentoring for both mentor and mentee, through a sharing of experiences, offering fresh perspectives, and exchanging ideas and guidance on different situations and objectives. That said, informal mentoring can sometimes be unbalanced, as a result of occurring in an organic/ad hoc manner and not being available to everyone who may be interested in having a mentor. Sometimes mentors gravitate to junior members of the organization who remind them of themselves when they began their careers, which can potentially result in favoritism and similarity bias. Therefore, a structured mentoring program is often the most effective and fair in approach, allowing everyone to sign up for the opportunity to be mentored or be a mentor, with pragmatic and relevant pairing of mentor with mentee. Additionally, a structured mentoring program can include goal setting, action planning, and other key elements aligned with organizational talent management and career development strategies.

Management and executive coaching is similar to mentoring, typically a one-on-one professional relationship providing advice and guidance. The difference is the recipient of this type of coaching is already in a senior-level managerial/leadership role, typically working with a certified coach with leadership-specific expertise rather than an internal member of the organization. Many organizations retain executive and management coaches in a consultative manner, engaging them as needed to offer senior leaders the opportunity to learn new strategies and acquire new or trending knowledge and skills.

8.3.4 Experiential and Hands-on Learning

Experiential learning can be acquired through different types of actual experiences, either on-the-job in real time or delivered in a simulated scenario. We will explore several approaches that demonstrate value within a leadership development strategy: stretch and special assignments, job rotation and job shadowing, and assessment centers.

Stretch and Special Assignments

Stretch and special assignments provide a more high-impact work experience that activities occurring in an educational class may not provide. These type of hands-on assignments offer the opportunity to gain real and tangible experience in a new or more challenging area (i.e., 'stretching' oneself for growth). Real-world learning experiences, both personally and professionally, stay with us in a more profound way because we have lived them. We can recall our behaviors and actions, the outcomes, and how they affected us both positively and negatively. These 'life lessons' can then be applied to other circumstances and situations. The effectiveness of such assignments is contingent on factors including the degree of challenge and complexity of the assignment, a climate that allows for risk-taking and mistake-making without negative consequences, and the quality of support and feedback received from one's manager without micromanagement (Yukl, 1998).

Job Rotation and Job Shadowing

Individuals in a job rotation work in different functional areas or departments for a specified time frame and are given a variety of work tasks to perform while they interact with new people during each cycle of the rotation. This is a good opportunity to obtain new knowledge and skills, apply existing knowledge and skills in new and different ways, and build one's professional network through expanded cross-functional collaboration. With job shadowing, an individual will follow an experienced leader during the course of their work routine in a 'day in the life' type of scenario or will follow them for observation through a specific type of task or responsibility (e.g., running a meeting). While the learner may participate in some small way, they are typically just observing the leader or senior-level person performing certain aspects of their job.

Assessment Centers

While the name assessment 'center' implies an actual physical location, they are really a multifaceted strategy that integrates various methods and techniques for leadership/management performance evaluation and development. An assessment center is an excellent approach for roles with complex performance dimensions and elements of criticality, high-risk, and/or a high level of responsibility (Picardi, 2019). An additional benefit is that the same methods can be leveraged for leader and manager selection and hiring or promotion decisions. An assessment center program is often comprised of an array of activities designed to assess an individual's proficiency and ability to perform relevant tasks, including hands-on simulation exercises, work samples, hypothetical scenarios and case studies, role-play, presentations, and live group discussions. Because the roles considered appropriate for an assessment center will have complex and multifaceted responsibilities, many activities will naturally encompass several performance dimensions simultaneously as they would occur in actual on-the-job situations. While assessment centers can be valuable and provide a strong return on investment (ROI) for the organization, their implementation will depend on available resources, including budget, time, people effort/ expertise, and logistical/technical requirements.

No matter what the leadership development goals are or the combination of approaches implemented, there should be a strategic plan in place that integrates current and projected future needs, existing knowledge, skills, and abilities, and competencies needed to continue to achieve performance goals and organizational objectives. No one process can succeed on its own in a silo and must be part of a comprehensive strategy. In our final section of this chapter, we will consider some best practices for the design, implementation, and evaluation of leadership development programs and initiatives.

8.4 Leadership Development Best Practices

An organizational culture that embraces ongoing leadership development opportunities and enables its members to make progress towards their professional goals and highest potential will be able to sustain a competent, capable, and confident workforce positioned to lead effectively today and in the future.

A comprehensive strategy is essential for success, comprised of many of the best practices outlined below.

- Design clear learning objectives based on thorough knowledge and skills needs assessment and aligned with desired and expected performance outcomes.

- Create clear, focused content appropriate to the level of the learner audience and logically sequenced.

- Deliver each program through the appropriate delivery modality or combination of multiple modalities based on factors such as time frame, logistical parameters, and geographic dispersion of learners.

- Integrate hands-on training elements and other active learning methods for practice and immediate feedback.

- Supply resources, post-program reference tools, and offer follow-up opportunities to answer questions or provide additional feedback.

- Encourage leaders and managers to support their group members after the program, allowing them to apply new knowledge and skills on the job and offering feedback and guidance to sustain continued performance.

- Coach learners to take initiative in their developmental experience and not to rely exclusively on passively receiving information and resources, but to proactively seek out assistance, advice, materials, and feedback.

- Encourage a mindset of continuous growth by staying abreast of trends, current issues, and best practices, as well as networking with other leaders and professionals for knowledge sharing.

Leadership development efforts should be clearly aligned with an organization's performance management and career development strategies. The success of any leadership development strategy is dependent on the organizational culture, values, and conditions that support the investment in budgetary and other resources to provide diverse and ongoing growth opportunities, as well as support for individuals to demonstrate new competencies in their current roles and position themselves for future leadership roles.

Chapter Summary

◆ The development and maintenance of a leadership development strategy is essential for organizations to facilitate the knowledge and skill acquisition, coaching, and growth essential to prepare individuals for roles of increased leadership responsibility.

◆ Succession planning is a strategic long-range process for identifying and developing individuals to advance into leadership/management roles as current leaders plan to vacate their respective roles over time, ensuring continuity and minimizing loss of knowledge and expertise.

◆ A competency model is used to describe actionable behaviors necessary for achieving specified performance outcomes and goals, and can be an integral part of assessing learning and development needs.

◆ A leadership development strategy can integrate different approaches depending on needs and goals, including formal degree and certificate programs, workshops and classes, mentoring and coaching, and experiential and hands-on learning opportunities.

◆ The success of any leadership development strategy is dependent on the organizational culture, values, and conditions that support the investment in budgetary and other resources to provide continuous learning along with diverse and ongoing growth opportunities.

Quiz 8

1. The strategic process of developing individuals for future placement in leadership/management roles in preparation for existing leaders and managers to vacate their respective positions is referred to as _____.

   a. talent management

   b. succession planning

   c. leader transference

   d. leadership planning

2. Which of the following Lominger Competency categories would be most closely aligned with the ability to evaluate performance outcomes and implement metrics to gather information regarding key performance indicators (KPI's), effectiveness, and efficiency?

   a. Managing and Measuring Work

   b. Organizational Agility

   c. Innovation Management

   d. Priority Setting

3. A manager that finds it challenging to work through projects with minimal instructions and vague expectations would likely need development in which of the following Lominger Competency categories?

   a. Managerial Courage

   b. Innovation Management

   c. Dealing With Ambiguity

   d. Process Management

4. Which of the following leadership development methods integrates multiple activities, including hands-on simulation exercises, hypothetical scenario analysis, role play, presentations, and group discussions?

   a. High Impact Learning

   b. On-the-job Training

   c. Mentoring Programs

   d. Assessment Centers

5. The _____ approach provides the opportunity to gain
   new knowledge, build skills, and interact with others by
   working in different departments/functions over the course
   of a specific time cycle.

   a. job shadowing

   b. job rotation

   c. job enrichment

   d. job coaching

Solutions to the above questions can be downloaded from
the **Online Resources** *section of this book on*
www.vibrantpublishers.com

Chapter 9

Ethical Leadership

A leader possesses a visible and impactful role, creating a need and opportunity to demonstrate their integrity, work ethic, and positive, moral values through their daily decisions and behaviors. For every decision that a leader makes, there will always be some type of ethical component with positive and negative implications to various stakeholder groups such as employees, customers, investors, and the public. A leader acting with integrity and a sound moral compass will determine the decisions and actions that will result in ethical outcomes. A leader has a critical responsibility to uphold moral principles, integrity, and justice, as they strive to provide the most beneficial outcomes for their stakeholders as possible with minimal or no negative consequences.

In this chapter, we examine the concept of ethics in leadership including the definition of ethics, factors that influence ethical and unethical behavior, and the principles and best practices of ethical leadership.

After reading this chapter, key learning objectives attained will include:

- Understanding the definition of ethics, and the implications of ethical and unethical behaviors on positive and negative consequences to others.

- Describing the importance of ethics in leadership roles, and the critical need for leaders to make decisions and take actions based on guiding ethical principles and values.

- Analyzing theories that depict the extent to which a leader's concern for self-interests versus their concern for others' interests will influence their ethical behavior.

- Examining the factors that may impact a leader's likelihood to act unethically, including their individual traits, the nature of the followers, and the environment or situation.

- Assessing the principles and best practices for effective and ethical leadership in an array of contexts.

9.1 Ethics Defined

Before we explore ethical leadership, let's first review the concept of ethics. Ethics consists of the values, beliefs, and practices of an individual, group, or society that are deemed virtuous, morally correct, and acceptable in that environment or setting (Northouse, 2016). An individual's morals and values influence the extent to which their decisions and actions are ethical. While ethical practices and legal practices can overlap, they are not always the same. An action may be legal but not ethical, in that no laws are being broken but the action is not morally acceptable and is causing one or more individuals some degree of harm that can be avoided. We cannot assume that legal and ethical practices are always the same in all circumstances. Some examples of behaviors that are ubiquitously perceived as unethical but may differ in terms of legality include hypocrisy, dishonesty, sabotage, revenge, greediness, prejudice, harassment, and deception.

Acting ethically is also referred to as acting with integrity. The concept of integrity refers to the ability to demonstrate one's ethical principles, to 'practice what you preach' regardless of the circumstance.

When considering the extent to which one acts with integrity in a given situation, the following questions can be considered:

1. Does this action 'feel' like the right thing to do?

2. Is this action as fair as possible to others?

3. Is anyone harmed, or does the action infringe upon anyone's rights?

4. Would you recommend this decision or action to someone else if they faced the same situation?

5. Will you be able to 'put your head on your pillow' tonight after enacting this decision today?

(Dubrin, 2007)

While ethical behavior is clearly a vitally important element for everyone to understand and integrate in their daily lives, ethics is especially important for leaders to embrace and demonstrate due to the powerful and influential nature of their role. In the next section, we will examine the impact of ethics in leadership roles.

9.2 Ethics in Leadership

The decisions, behaviors, and actions of leaders should clearly and consistently support the purpose and mission of their group or organization, be clearly aligned with shared values, and support and/or contribute to societal improvement, justice, and corporate social responsibility which refers to the effort of going above and beyond organizational goals in ways that benefit and serve external communities. The reality is, this is easier said than done. It becomes an ongoing balancing act in terms of producing the most effective and desirable outcomes without causing any individuals or groups distress or negative consequences. For those of you who may have held a leader position or role, you probably understand this challenge. While every leader will have a strategic plan, agenda, or goals that may not align perfectly with every follower, they do have an obligation to everyone to ensure their plans are not dangerous, harmful, or produce hardship for their followers.

To sustain this level of responsibility to their stakeholders, all leaders should have the knowledge and skills to assess their own tendencies and the resulting differences in ethical consequences. Researchers (Bowie, 1991; Schumann, 2001; Avolio & Locke, 2002) have developed several ethical theories based on their research findings that can be used for this type of assessment. These theories, highlighted in Table 9.1, center around three distinct approaches to understanding the ethical consequences of decision making and differ on two key dimensions: concern for self-interests and concern for others' interests.

Table 9.1

Theory	Concern for Self-Interests	Concern for Others' Interests
Ethical Egoism Individual acts to create the greatest good for themselves	High	Low
Utilitarianism Individual acts to create the greatest good for the group(s) with the greatest number	Moderate	Moderate
Altruism Individual acts to create the greatest good for others with little focus on self-interests	Low	High

(Bowie, 1991; Schumann, 2001; Avolio & Locke, 2002)

These theories hold value for leadership development, particularly in the area of self-awareness and understanding the far-reaching impact of a leader's decisions and actions. Leaders must develop and sustain the ability to successfully balance needs that will directly benefit themselves with the needs of others as well as the community as a whole, and be prepared to make their own interests and goals a lesser priority if necessary. They must have strength of character and conviction to avoid the lure of desirable immediate gains such as profitability and competitiveness at the expense of quality, fairness, transparency, honesty, safety, and sustainability. By striving to achieve these short-term gains while simultaneously acting in the best interest of their followers, group members, and external constituents, a leader will demonstrate ethical principles and act in a socially responsible manner that will have both short and long-term benefits for everyone, including themselves. Research by Heifetz (1994) proposed that ethical leaders must maintain a safe and stable environment for their followers or group members so they feel supported as they face their own day-to-day dilemmas and ethical challenges to navigate appropriately. An ethical leader will offer a sound moral compass and serve as a reliable example through change, and conflicting situations to ensure followers stay on the ethical path together. Followers or group members should also be inspired to act in the same manner because they see the benefit and impact of behaving with integrity through the leader's example and wish to support their shared values and ethical conduct. They must be able to trust the leader to be in charge, guide and engage the group, make decisions, and take actions in the best interest of everyone involved as well as the organization. This is the leader's moral responsibility to their followers or group members.

There are myriad factors that can affect an individual's likelihood to lead ethically and with integrity. In the next section, we will examine these factors and the extent to which they may influence a leader to act ethically or unethically.

9.3 Factors Influencing Ethical Leadership

The reality is that no leader will demonstrate sound ethical behavior 100% of the time. Sometimes unethical decisions are made without fully realizing the extent of their consequences to others, so there can be a degree of trial and error when striving to lead ethically. That said, there are a variety of factors that may influence the likelihood of ethical or unethical decisions and behaviors, as highlighted below.

- Individual moral development, environment of one's upbringing.

- Individual traits and attributes.

- Concern or fear of failure to meet expectations.

- Perception of insecurity regarding the extent of one's power/control.

- Sense of entitlement in one's role/position.

- Situational/contextual factors such as organizational culture, conformity/peer pressure, demands of others.

There is a misconception that some of these individualized elements are either innate or cannot be changed. Moral values and practices can be learned, accepted, and practiced at any stage of life. Decisions, behaviors, and actions can be in alignment with a moral compass and ethical code of conduct and principles that an individual may develop over time through learning, expanding self-awareness, and developing empathy and emotional intelligence. The latter three factors – perception of power/control, sense of position-based entitlement, and situational/contextual factors – may actually result in a leader's likelihood to abuse the power and influence that comes with their role, and this is a particularly important consideration that requires a deeper assessment.

Abuse of Power and Influence

Leaders inherently have a level of power and influence that often surpasses their followers or group members. This is the nature of the leader-follower relationship. With power and influence comes great responsibility for a leader to respect the extent of their potential control and influence on their followers. Unfortunately, power can be addictive and having some power may motivate an individual to desire more and/or additional types of power. There will often be a variety of factors contributing to a leader's abuse of power, including (1) the leader's potential for ego-driven and self-serving behavior, (2) the nature and characteristics of their followers, and (3) the environment or specific situation. A leader that prioritizes their own personal agenda and self-interests at the expense of others including their group, the organization, and external stakeholders is more likely to resort to unethical behavior and abuse of power. Followers that are passive or vulnerable may be more easily manipulated and made to feel dependent on the leader for all their outcomes. An environment that is unstable, lacking clear values, and without a sense of direction, or lacking checks and balances may result in followers not knowing what each day will bring in terms of the leader's decisions and actions on behalf of the group (i.e., 'keep them guessing'). These factors comprise what is known as the toxic triangle, a concept developed by researchers Padilla, Hogan, and Keiser (2007). The likelihood of unethical leader behavior and abuse of power will depend on the prevalence of one or more of these factors existing within the organizational structure.

In an organizational context, leaders and managers can sometimes perceive themselves to lack adequate power and control in their role, resulting in power hoarding, manipulation of their followers, and other tactics to acquire as much power as possible, sometimes through unethical means. Respected leadership and management expert Rosabeth Moss Kanter shared findings on perceived powerlessness and power abuse in her paper, 'Power Failure in Management Circuits' (Harvard Business

Review, 1979), including leader/manager insecurity in their position, lack of organizational support in the leader role, and lack of resources to enable effectiveness with their group in directing work and accomplishing goals. According to Kanter, effective and ethical use of power among leaders must be supported by an organization's culture, which is achieved through integrating several key elements:

- Having organizational resources and processes that enable leaders to lead without excessive rules and hindering boundaries.

- Providing leadership coaching and development to ensure leaders are secure and confident in their roles and understand how to apply their power and influence ethically and respectfully.

- Encouraging top-level leaders to empower mid-level leaders to make decisions and have an appropriate level of control over their respective areas.

- Supporting mid-level leaders to treat their staff members as valuable resources, empowering them and encouraging their input and contribution without perceiving staff as a threat or worrying about losing their own position power with the group.

Kanter asserts that with these elements in place, power is shared in a responsible and strategic way that will result in greater success, growth, and inclusion at all organizational levels. This is an effort that requires ethics that are integrated into visible actions and practices on a daily basis. In our last section of this chapter, we will explore best practices of ethical leadership.

9.4 Best Practices in Ethical Leadership

An ethical and responsible leader must have organizational support and shared, clearly aligned values for the leader to effectively demonstrate those values through their visible behaviors and actions for followers to believe in, support, and emulate. An array of ethical best practices are highlighted below, and many of them will be familiar because they are also part of transformational leadership.

- **Leading by Example**

  - Acting as a role model, accessible for followers to align with and adopt in their behaviors.

  - Conducting themselves professionally in all situations.

  - Demonstrating humility, not allowing ego to influence decisions and actions; selflessness.

  - Holding oneself accountable for the performance, outcomes, and results on behalf of the group or organization.

  - Fostering trust and loyalty by being accessible to followers and dependable by keeping promises.

- **Demonstrating Integrity**

  - Treating everyone with respect, compassion, and dignity, aware of followers' needs, interests, and concerns.

  - Refraining from exploiting, manipulating, or taking advantage of any followers or group members, avoiding unethical influence tactics such as guilt, peer pressure, ingratiation, harassment, and coercion.

- Making decisions that followers perceive as just, correct, and morally sound.

- Integrating shared values into decisions made and actions taken.

- Maintaining resilience through challenges, without resorting to easy/unethical alternatives.

- Acting with generosity and a spirit of giving to others.

- **Diplomacy and Civic Relations**

  - Communicating with honesty and straightforwardness.

  - Demonstrating transparency with no hidden agendas.

  - Having empathy for others; seeing a situation through the lens of others and understanding their needs and point of view.

  - Maintaining objectivity and unbiased perspectives.

  - Supporting inclusion in which no one is left out or excluded within the group.

  - Handling conflict through fair and rational resolution approaches.

- **Focus**

  - Maintaining appropriate attention to short and long-term goals along with needs that arise unpredictably (i.e., 'keeping all the balls up in the air').

  - Demonstrating self-control and discipline in completing tasks and making progress on meeting objectives.

  - Avoiding spreading oneself and the group too thin which may lead to compromising behaviors.

- Remaining firm on values and position, not easily persuaded or influenced to shift towards someone else's agenda that deviates from the mission to serve the greater good

When these behaviors and practices are all integrated, they comprise a true depiction of ethical leadership, comprehensively organized within five core principles of ethical leadership (Northouse, 2016), described in Table 9.2 below. These principles are relevant and applicable to leaders in all types of circumstances and facets of society. They provide a solid foundation from which organizations, businesses, government, education, healthcare, nonprofit, and other entities/institutions can build and add more niche/specific elements for a holistic model for practical implementation.

Table 9.2

Ethical Leadership Principle	Principle Description
Build Community	<ul><li>A compelling vision and purpose</li><li>Shared values and common goals that benefit everyone involved in a meaningful way</li><li>Support for community sustainability and growth, serving the public interest as much as possible</li></ul>
Respect Others	<ul><li>Facilitation of mutual respect and professionalism among everyone</li><li>Encouragement for followers' to share their uniqueness and authenticity; respect for diversity</li></ul>
Serve Others	<ul><li>A duty to prioritize the welfare of others over goals; attention to the needs of all stakeholders</li><li>Treatment of others with beneficence</li></ul>
Show Justice	<ul><li>Fairness and appropriateness of decisions made</li><li>Clear and acceptable rationale provided for decisions, supporting and upholding the rights of others</li></ul>
Demonstrate Honesty	<ul><li>Truthful, open communication, transparency and information sharing</li><li>No omission or hidden agendas</li></ul>

(Northouse, 2016)

While it may require substantial effort for a leader to balance ethics with all the responsibilities and expectations of their role, it is a critical component of long-term effectiveness and sustainability. Stakeholders expect leaders, in all areas of society, to willingly demonstrate all of the behaviors and actions discussed in this chapter, and to be ready to resolve any issues that may result from inadvertently acting in an unethical manner. With ethical leadership in place, organizations have the capability to sustain their own success and growth while at the same time, making significant and positive changes that benefit the greater good.

Chapter Summary

◆ Ethics is comprised of the values, beliefs, and practices of an individual, group, or society that are perceived as morally correct and acceptable to everyone in a particular environment.

◆ Theories relevant to ethical behavior center around three distinct approaches to understanding the ethical consequences of decision making and differ on two key dimensions: concern for self-interests and concern for others' interests.

◆ Leaders must have the ability to successfully balance needs that will directly benefit themselves with the needs of others as well as the community as a whole, and to be prepared to make their own interests and goals a lesser priority if necessary.

◆ With power and influence comes great responsibility for a leader to respect the extent of their potential control and influence on their followers. Several factors contributing to a leader's abuse of power include (1) the leader's potential for ego-driven and self-serving behavior, (2) the nature and characteristics of their followers, and (3) the environment/situation.

◆ When ethical behaviors and practices are integrated, they comprise a true depiction of ethical leadership, organized within five core principles of ethical leadership: building community, respecting others, serving others, showing justice, and demonstrating honesty.

Quiz 9

1. The concept of _____ is concerned with an organization's efforts to serve external community or population's needs in altruistic ways that go beyond what may benefit the organization itself.

    a. collaborative leadership

    b. corporate social responsibility

    c. community innovation

    d. contingency management

2. Which of the following behaviors is not a common ethical challenge for leaders?

    a. Withholding necessary information

    b. Failing to report safety violations

    c. Making shareholders' needs a priority

    d. Fabricating financial report data

3. According to ethics theory, a leader that demonstrates high concern for self-interests and low concern for others' interests would most likely be exhibiting which concept?

    a. Moral Leadership

    b. Ethical Egoism

    c. Altruism

    d. Utilitarianism

4. A leader that shares values and common goals that benefit everyone involved in a meaningful way is demonstrating which ethical leadership principle?

   a. Build Community

   b. Respect Others

   c. Show Justice

   d. Demonstrate Honesty

5. When a leader supports and upholds the rights of others, they are most likely demonstrating which ethical leadership principle?

   a. Demonstrate Honesty

   b. Show Justice

   c. Respect Others

   d. Build Community

Solutions to the above questions can be downloaded from
the **Online Resources** *section of this book on*
www.vibrantpublishers.com

This page is intentionally left blank

Chapter **10**

Leading a Thriving Organization

Throughout this book we have examined the breadth and complexity of all the different needs, challenges, expectations, and goals that leaders must address and manage effectively. It is clear that strong, proactive, and impactful leaders are essential now more than ever and will continue to be a vital role among all areas of society in the future.

In this final chapter of the book, we examine several key areas of focus, specifically managing change, leading through crisis, and demonstrating global competency, which have emerged as a result of trends and shifting needs that require strategic planning and action from leaders in all roles and scenarios.

After reading this chapter, key learning objectives attained will include:

- Explaining the importance of change management and the strategies a leader can use to facilitate sustainable

change that is supported by their followers and
stakeholders.

- Describing the concept of crisis leadership and the
  unique attributes necessary for leading others through
  a crisis situation.

- Analyzing examples of leaders who have demonstrated
  exemplary crisis leadership in different adverse
  circumstances.

- Assessing the unique competencies that are required
  for effective global leadership.

10.1 Trends Impacting Leadership

Trends and shifts in various facets of society will continue
to evolve and require responsive leaders ready and willing to
adapt and direct their followers accordingly. Such trends as
technological advancement, economic fluctuation, governmental/
political instability, social reform awareness, and global public
health/welfare issues have resulted in essential focus areas for
leaders, including:

- Managing Continuous Change

- Leading Through Crisis Situations

- Demonstrating Global Competency

In the sections that follow, each of these areas will be examined
in depth to fully understand how effective leadership will need

to evolve to serve current and future shifts, challenges, and stakeholder expectations.

10.2 Leading Change

Leaders, regardless of specific role or setting, will face ongoing change and are expected to make strategic decisions in response to shifting needs that may be planned or unexpected. Additionally, sometimes leaders will be required to make decisions and take actions without clear or sufficient information and/or resources. The outcomes for affected stakeholders will depend on how effective a leader can stay on top of changes and navigate through varying circumstances as they direct their followers towards positive and productive results. Sometimes followers will adapt quickly and willingly support the leader's direction, and other times followers will need a bit more influence and explanation to fully support the leader's position and plan for managing the change. Followers may be resistant to change at times despite the leader providing appropriate rationale and mapping out a reasonable plan. A leader must be able to handle any scenario because their followers or group members' adaptability will be necessary for a successful outcome.

Why are followers sometimes resistant to change, even when their admired and/or respected leader is requesting their support? The main reason is that change requires that individuals and groups adapt to new conditions and adjust their behaviors to meet the needs of different circumstances and expectations, which may not always be appealing or easy. There are many other reasons, some valid and some not, but it is important to remember that individuals or groups may not be resisting the change in a malicious or sabotaging way, but in protection and defense of their own needs and interests. While every situation will have different circumstances, resistance to change may be due to one or more of the following influencing factors:

- A mistrustful environment.

- Belief that the proposed change is not really necessary.

- Perceived loss or hardship based on unknown future outcomes.

- Fear of failure due to not being set up for success.

- The proposed change goes against individual or group values.

- Unclear goals/expectations.

- Unrealistic goals/objectives that are not perceived as feasible.

- Belief that the costs of the change will outweigh any benefits.

- Individual protection of self-interests (WIIFM).

Despite potential resistance, a leader must find a strategy for gaining follower support and moving forward to manage necessary change because the group or organization's future success or even existence may depend on adapting to this change. An effective first step is for a leader to identify any followers who are supportive and demonstrate readiness for change as their support system and change agents, which may facilitate greater acceptance of the change from the rest of the group. From there, a leader can integrate an array of strategies and best practices for directing and navigating the group through each step of the change. Yukl (1998) identified key leader behaviors and approaches for facilitating change, as highlighted below:

- Communicate regularly with transparency, reiterating the need for change, the sense of urgency, the new vision and positive outcomes, and how group members will be integral to the change effort.

- Describe the decisions and actions that will be implemented and provide ongoing and proactive status updates, changes to the plan, progress made, and next steps.

- Be accessible and available for followers or group members to ask questions and share concerns.

- Explain how the benefits of the change will outweigh the costs, using examples as specific and relevant to followers' interests as possible (WIIFM).

- Provide as much support and validation as necessary that everyone will be taken care of as best as possible to minimize disruption or negative outcomes.

- Coordinate representatives across all functions/levels to act as liaisons, facilitating two-way communication between the leader and their respective areas to garner support and trust.

- Create strategic teams and committees, each assigned specific goals that integrate with the big picture.

- Provide information, tools, training, coaching, and other resources to set everyone up for success as they adjust to changes in their respective roles.

- Empower everyone in some capacity, giving individuals the opportunity to feel involved and contribute input which will increase investment and support.

- Emphasize that a beneficial outcome to dealing with change and stepping out of one's comfort zone is increased resiliency and adaptability which is a positive attribute for everyone.

A valuable tool that a leader can use to help anticipate potential needs for future change or navigate a change that currently exists is called a SWOT analysis. The acronym SWOT stands for strengths, weaknesses, opportunities, and threats, described in Table 10.1. The benefits of a SWOT analysis is, it is not costly to perform, is not overly complex or time-consuming, and can offer new insights to leaders in terms of how to assess current and future circumstances and consider their decisions and actions in the most appropriate and effective manner.

Table 10.1

Strengths	• Areas of competence, knowledge skills, and abilities • Existing attributes/elements that offer a competitive advantage • Tangible assets such as geographic location, infrastructure, access to capital and other resources
Weaknesses	• Gaps or deficits in necessary competencies, knowledge, skills, and abilities • Areas that are lacking in order to maintain competitiveness • Insufficient resources and/or inability to secure necessary assets and resources
Opportunities	• Ability to produce and/or innovate with agility and responsiveness • Knowledge of future circumstances that may open up potential for growth • Few competitors
Threats	• Shifting trends or stakeholder needs that will be difficult to accommodate • Tightening or reduction of access to resources • Many or emerging competitors

There are many different tools, worksheets, and templates available for developing a SWOT analysis. By mapping out each of these areas side by side and reviewing them in this comprehensive manner, a leader can clearly identify areas in need of greater focus and assessment to sustain continued success and/or work through a challenging situation, which every leader must face. Leading through challenging, crisis situations often defines a leader as they handle circumstances that test their limits of effectiveness and strength, which is the focus of the next section.

10.3 Crisis Leadership

A crisis situation is often a sudden and unexpected circumstance that brings about disruption and negative outcomes for many individuals or groups. Crisis situations can stem from environmental/natural disasters, economic shifts, acts of violence/ terrorism, political turmoil, social unrest, public health, and safety emergencies, to name a few examples. Regardless of the type of crisis, a strong leader will be critical to direct and move followers and stakeholders out of the situation quickly and take swift action to resolve the crisis with minimal disruption and negative consequences as possible. This requires a leader to think rationally, know how to mobilize key support, thoroughly troubleshoot, and act decisively while also demonstrating emotional stability, compassion, and empathy. A leader handling a crisis must know the risks involved with each option in front of them, act as prudently and responsibly, and also as quickly as possible for the greater good. Below are several examples of organizational crisis situations and the leaders that addressed and resolved them with great effectiveness.

1. General Motors (GM)

In 2014, Mary Barra, the company's first female CEO, was faced with a significant defect in the ignition switch vehicle mechanism after being in the CEO role for only two months. She was quickly faced with managing a major recall, ensuring public safety as best as possible, and averting a public relations issue. She swiftly issued a public statement and took responsibility for the problem as well as the steps being taken to resolve it. The accountability won her favor in the eyes of the public, consumers, investors, and the GM workforce.

(Hall, 2018)

2. JetBlue

In 2007, an ice storm in the U.S. Northeast forced JetBlue to cancel over 1000 flights despite its policy to 'never' cancel flights. Stranded passengers were stuck in airports for days which prompted a social media frenzy of complaints that threatened the company's future. JetBlue's CEO, David Neeleman, responded quickly and took full responsibility for the issue, not even blaming the severe weather for the operational breakdown. He delivered a live statement and public apology on television and internet media outlets as well as a written statement and plan for compensating all customers impacted by the cancellations. Even though the crisis cost JetBlue millions of dollars, Neeleman's efforts saved the company and its reputation.

(Hall, 2018)

3. Johnson & Johnson

In 1982, the unthinkable occurred in the U.S. – bottles of Johnson & Johnson's popular product Extra Strength Tylenol were purposely laced with cyanide, resulting in the poisoning deaths of seven people. This crisis quickly escalated into a national public health and safety panic. The CEO at that time, James Burke, knew he had to respond immediately to ensure public safety and eliminate the chance of anyone else ingesting a contaminated product, but also take responsibility to address the nation and quell their fear and anxiety. Burke took immediate action to remove more than 32 million bottles of Tylenol products from store shelves, pharmacies, and medical centers. He gave a public apology and took full responsibility for the crisis, which became the catalyst for introducing improved public and consumer health protocol, product safety seals, and other safeguards that we see today on an array of consumer products. The Tylenol tragedy could have easily resulted in the end for Johnson & Johnson, but Burke led the company through the crisis with compassion and effectiveness and restored quality control, standards of excellence, consumer trust, and brand reputation.

(Hall, 2018)

While there are many examples of organizational leaders who have demonstrated excellent crisis management in different situations, these examples showcase a common theme of leader traits and behaviors that are important not only in resolving the crisis situation but also dealing with its impact. They all were extraordinarily responsive and empathetic to the perceptions and needs of their stakeholders, they proactively communicated an appropriate message with transparency, took full accountability of the situation, and assured the public that a plan of action was being implemented to resolve the issue as rapidly as possible with the least amount of hardship or further negative consequence to anyone. Even when a crisis is specific to a particular setting or location, it will impact and ripple out to broader areas in different ways which makes proactive and widespread communication, often on a global scale, a vital action. Our final section of this chapter examines the importance of leading in a global context and the criticality of global leadership competencies.

10.4 Global Leadership

As our world becomes increasingly connected and global alliances and partnerships evolve in new and impactful ways, leaders need to be effective in terms of their leadership strategies and behaviors while also demonstrating a set of global competencies as they plan, direct, and interact/collaborate with individuals and groups from a diverse array of countries and regions. Leaders must be knowledgeable and well-informed about different countries and global regions in order to accomplish their goals and objectives that ultimately result in achieving their vision and mission. While it may be unrealistic to expect a leader to fully understand all of the differences among every geographic area worldwide, it is important to have the tools and resources with which to examine the unique facets of a country, its culture, and how it may be similar or different from other areas. Perhaps the most widely-recognized researcher in the field of global cultural differences is Geert Hofstede (1980), who developed the following five global cultural dimensions that will vary among countries and global regions:

Power Distance

The power distance dimension refers to the acceptance of a hierarchical structure and distribution of power that may be unequally distributed, as well as respect for individuals in positions or roles of a higher hierarchical level.

Uncertainty Avoidance

The uncertainty avoidance dimension refers to the extent to which a culture easily handles ambiguity, its comfort level with risk, unpredictability, the unknown, and its dependence on social norms, protocol and structured rules to behave with stability and predictability.

Individualism – Collectivism

The individualism-collectivism dimension refers to the extent to which the individuals in a culture behave in a manner that is self-serving and competitive, fulfilling an individualistic goal or agenda, or in a manner that is family or team-oriented and cooperative, with their efforts benefiting the entire group.

Masculinity – Femininity

The masculinity-femininity dimension refers to the extent to which a country's culture emphasizes assertive, competitive, and achievement-oriented behaviors or more cooperative, supportive, and nurturing behaviors.

Long-term – Short-term Orientation

The long-term-short-term orientation dimension refers to the extent to which a culture prioritizes immediate and present needs and desires or maintains a focus on long-term goals and objectives through strategic planning and preparation for the future.

The value of Hofstede's global cultural dimensions is that having an awareness of the attributes of different country cultures can facilitate a better understanding of and respect for their behavioral norms and expectations, their accepted organizational practices, and the leadership attributes and behaviors most effective in that culture. These globally-appropriate attributes and behaviors can then be developed in leaders, with specific focus on certain countries or regions in which the leader is involved or planning to be more involved. There is a great deal of valuable research in the area of global leadership competencies. Researchers Adler and Bartholomew (1992) developed a set of cultural competencies for improving one's global awareness, respect, and understanding, including:

1. Knowledge of business, political, and cultural environments worldwide.

2. Understanding of and openness to cultural differences in perspectives, tastes/preferences, trends, and technologies.

3. Ability to work effectively with individuals and groups from an array of diverse cultures.

4. Adaptability to living, working, and communicating in different global cultures.

5. Ability to respect and relate to individuals and groups in different cultures with equality.

Global leadership research findings have also provided a means to organize the various competencies into logical categories for ease in conducting needs assessments and designing leadership development programs. The Thunderbird School of Global Management is a world-renowned institution within Arizona State University, comprised of researchers with a focus on the concept of global mindset (Javidan, Hough, & Bullough, 2010).

They developed an assessment tool, the Global Mindset® Inventory, which is used to measure and predict performance in global leadership based on three main categories: intellectual capital, psychological capital, and social capital, as highlighted in Table 10.2.

Table 10.2

Intellectual Capital	Psychological Capital	Social Capital
Knowledge of complex global issues	Openness to cultural differences, traditions, customs, and norms	Respect for and interest in practices supporting diversity, equity, and inclusion
Knowledge of geography, history, demographics, economy of different countries	Willingness to learn and adapt, try new things	Engagement with others, a collaborator, connector, and relationship builder
Understanding of the societal implications (e.g., political, environmental, economic) of different world events	Comfortable in unfamiliar environments/ situations	Ability to communicate with diplomacy and tact

(Javidan, Hough, & Bullough, 2010)

Findings such as these on the impact of global competencies have continued to emerge and provide insights on how effective leadership should be defined and how it should evolve for long-term relevance. Another large-scale and highly respected research initiative has been conducted through the GLOBE research program. The GLOBE program, an acronym which stands for Global Leadership and Organizational Behavior Effectiveness, was initiated by leadership expert Robert House in 1991 and has involved hundreds of collaborating researchers over the years. Findings from their landmark publication, Culture, Leadership, and Organizations: The GLOBE Study of 62 Societies (House, Hanges, Javidan, Dorfman, and Gupta, 2004) provided important foundational research findings to understand global leadership and from which to build future research ideas and studies. GLOBE researchers have applied the work of Hofstede to create regional clusters of countries to more efficiently examine and compare the similarities and differences of the various cultural dimensions by global region. Today, GLOBE researchers continue to collect and analyze data worldwide, yielding insights and findings on the relationship between culture and leadership, the impact of global culture differences on leader behaviors and effectiveness, and emerging trends and patterns that require increased focus for organizations and different facets of society.

As we conclude our exploration of leadership essentials, let's revisit one of the most important elements: a leader cannot exist and function without followers. This relationship is a two-way, interactive partnership in which everyone needs to be clearly focused, engaged, and committed to uphold role expectations in support of their collective goals and objectives as envisioned by the leader. A careful balance of structured productivity and loyal collaboration is critical to achieving performance outcomes that benefit all involved. The concepts, strategies, and practices in this book can be effectively applied to any type of leadership role, context, or setting.

Chapter Summary

◆ Trends and shifts in different areas of society require responsive leaders ready and willing to adapt and direct their followers accordingly. Areas of increasing criticality and focus for leaders include managing change, leading through crisis situations, and demonstrating global competency.

◆ Leaders face constant change and are expected to make prudent yet swift decisions in response to shifting needs, often without clear or sufficient information and/or resources. An effective leader will anticipate and navigate change as they direct their followers towards adapting in a manner that will result in positive and productive outcomes.

◆ A crisis is a sudden and unexpected circumstance that produces disruption and negative outcomes for many individuals or groups, requiring a strong leader to direct everyone out of the situation quickly by taking swift action to resolve the crisis with minimal disruption and consequences to others as possible.

◆ As our world becomes increasingly connected and global alliances and partnerships evolve, leaders are needed who demonstrate a set of global competencies as they plan, direct, and interact/collaborate with individuals and groups from a diverse array of countries and regions.

Quiz 10

1. **When communicating information about a crisis situation to followers or group members, an effective leader should take which of the following actions?**

   a. Downplay the situation and inform the group that there is nothing of concern occurring

   b. Explain the situation to the group and the actions being taken to address it and provide updates

   c. Tell the group about the crisis and hold a daily meeting to gather ideas for solutions from members

   d. Hold off on communicating to the group about the crisis situation for as long as possible

2. **All of the following factors may contribute to resistance to change, with the exception of _____.**

   a. fear of unknown future outcomes

   b. lack of goal clarity

   c. perceived benefits outweigh costs

   d. protection of self-interests

3. **A country with a low tolerance for risk taking and making decisions with insufficient/unknown information is most likely demonstrating which of the following Hofstede cultural dimensions?**

   a. Low Power Distance

   b. High Uncertainty Avoidance

   c. Low Collectivism

   d. High Power Distance

4. **A country with a strong team orientation and focus on cooperative work that benefits the entire group is most likely demonstrating which of the following Hofstede cultural dimensions?**

   a. High Collectivism

   b. High Power Distance

   c. High Masculinity

   d. High Individualism

5. A leader with _____ capital will likely demonstrate an openness to learning about different cultures and interest in experiencing different elements of a country's culture, such as foods and activities.

   a. intellectual

   b. ethical

   c. psychological

   d. social

Solutions to the above questions can be downloaded from
the **Online Resources** *section of this book on*
www.vibrantpublishers.com

References

Adler, N.J., & Bartholomew, S. (1992). Managing globally competent people. Academy of Management Executive, 6, 52-65.

Allport, G.W., & Odbert, H.S. (1933). Trait-names: A psycho-lexical study. Psychological Monographs, 47, 171-220.

Avolio, B.J. (1999). Full Leadership Development: Building the Vital Forces in Organizations. Thousand Oaks, CA: Sage Publications.

Avolio, B.J., & Locke, E.E. (2002). Contrasting different philosophies of leader motivation: Altruism versus egoism. Leadership Quarterly, 13, 169-191.

Barrick, M.R., & Mount, M.K. (1991). The Big Five personality dimensions and job performance: A meta-analysis. Personnel Psychology, 44(1), 1-26.

Bass, B.M. (1985). Leadership and Performance Beyond Expectations. New York: Free Press.

Bass, B.M. (1990). Bass and Stogdill's Handbook of Leadership: A Survey of Theory and Research. New York: Free Press.

Blake, R.R., & Mouton, J.S. (1964). The Managerial Grid. Houston, TX: Gulf Publishing Company.

Blanchard, K.H. (1985). SLII®: A Situational Approach to Managing People. Escondido, CA: Blanchard Training and Development.

Bowers, D.G., & Seashore, S.E. (1966). Predicting organizational effectiveness with a four-factor theory of leadership. Administrative Science Quarterly, 11, 238-263.

Bowie, N.E. (1991). Challenging the egoistic paradigm. Business Ethics Quarterly, 1(1), 1-21.

Burns, J.M. (1978). Leadership. New York: Harper & Row.

Cattell, R.B. (1947). Confirmation and clarification of primary personality factors. Psychometrika, 12, 197-220.

Costa, P.T., Jr., & McCrae, R.R. (1988). From catalog to classification: Murray's needs and the five-factor model. Journal of Personality and Social Psychology, 55(2), 258-265.

Dansereau, F., Graen, G.B., & Haga, W. (1975). A vertical dyad linkage approach to leadership in formal organizations. Organizational Behavior and Human Performance, 13, 46-78.

Dubrin, A.J. (2007). Leadership: Research Findings, Practice, and Skills (5th Ed). Boston: Houghton Mifflin.

Fiedler, F.E. (1964). A contingency model of leadership effectiveness. In L. Berkowitz (Ed.), Advances in Experimental Social Psychology, New York: Academic Press.

Fiedler, F.E., Chemers, M.M., & Mahar, L. (1976). Improving Leadership Effectiveness. New York: John Wiley & Sons.

Fiske, D.W. (1949). Consistency of the factorial structures of personality ratings from different sources. Journal of Abnormal and Social Psychology, 44, 329-344.

Forsyth, D.R. (2010). Group Dynamics (5th Edition). Belmont, CA: Wadsworth Cengage Learning.

Goleman, D. (1995). Emotional Intelligence. New York: Bantam Books.

Graen, G., & Uhl-Bien, M. (1995). Relationship-based approach to leadership: Development of leader-member exchange (LMX) theory of leadership over 25 years. Leadership Quarterly, 6, 219-247.

Hackman, J.R. (2012). From causes to conditions in group research. Journal of Organizational Behavior, 33, 428-444.

Hall, B. (19 April 2018). 5 CEOs Who Successfully Weathered a Crisis. The Entrepreneur Fund, https://theentrepreneurfund.com/5-ceos-who-successfully-weathered-a-crisis/.

Heifetz, R.A. (1994). Leadership Without Easy Answers. Cambridge, MA: Harvard University Press.

Hersey, P., & Blanchard, K.H. (1969). Management of Organizational Behavior: Utilizing Human Resources. Englewood Cliffs, NJ: Prentice Hall.

Hersey, P., & Blanchard, K.H. (1977). Management of Organizational Behavior: Utilizing Human Resources (3rd Ed). Englewood Cliffs, NJ: Prentice Hall.

Hofstede, G. (1980). Culture's Consequences: Comparing Values, Behaviors, Institutions, and Organizations across Nations. Thousand Oaks, CA: Sage Publications Inc.

Hogan, R.T. (1991). Personality and personality measurement. In M.D. Dunnette & L.M. Hough (Eds.), Handbook of Industrial and Organizational Psychology (2nd Ed., Vol. 2, 873-919). Consulting Psychologists Press.

House, R.J. (1971). A path-goal theory of leader effectiveness. Administrative Science Quarterly, 16, 321-339.

House, R.J. (1977). A 1976 theory of charismatic leadership. Leadership: The Cutting Edge, Carbondale IL, pp. 189-207.

House, R.J., & Mitchell, T.R. (1974). Path-goal theory of leadership. Contemporary Business, 3 (Fall), 81-98.

House, R.J., Hanges, P.J., Javidan, M., Dorfman, P.W., & Gupta, V. (2004). Culture, Leadership, and Organizations: The GLOBE Study of 62 Societies. Thousand Oaks, CA: Sage Publications Inc.

Howell, J.M., & Avolio, B.J. (August 1998). Transformational leadership, transactional leadership, locus of control, and support for innovation: Key predictors of consolidated business unit performance. Academy of Management Journal, pp. 387-409.

Javidan, M., Hough, L., & Bullough, A. (2010). Conceptualizing and Measuring Global Mindset®: Development of the Global Mindset Inventory. Glendale, AZ: Thunderbird School of Global Management, Najafi Global Mindset Institute.

Judge, T. A., & Piccolo, R.F. (October 2004). Transformational and transactional leadership: A meta-analytic test of their relative validity. Journal of Applied Psychology, pp. 755-768.

Kahn, R.L. (1956). The prediction of productivity. Journal of Social Issues, 12, 41-49.

Kanter, R.M. (1979). Power failure in management circuits. Harvard Business Review, 57(4), 65-75.

Katz R.L. (1955). Skills of an effective administrator. Harvard Business Review, 33(1), 33-42.

Kipnis, D. (1976). The Powerholders. Chicago, IL: University of Chicago Press.

Kipnis, D., Schmidt, S., Swaffin-Smith, C., & Wilkinson, I. (1984). Patterns of managerial influence: Shotgun managers, tacticians, and bystanders. Organizational Dynamics, 12(3), 58-67.

Kurz, R., & Bartram, D. (2002). Competency and individual performance: Modeling the world of work. In I.T. Robertson, M. Callinan, & D. Bartram (Eds.), Organizational Effectiveness: The Role of Psychology (pp. 227-255). Hoboken, NJ: John Wiley & Sons, Ltd.

Larson, C.E., & LaFasto, F.M.J. (1989). Teamwork: What Must Go Right/What Can Go Wrong. Newbury Park, CA: Sage Publications Inc.

Liden, R.C., Wayne, S.J., & Stilwell, D. (1993). A longitudinal study on the early development of leader-member exchange. Journal of Applied Psychology, 78, 662-674.

Levi, D. (2017). Group Dynamics for Teams (5th Ed). Thousand Oaks, CA: Sage Publications Inc.

Lombardo, M. & Eichinger, (1998). FYI: For Your Improvement, A Development and Coaching Guide (2nd Ed). Lominger Ltd, Inc.

McCauley, C., Ruderman, M., Ohlott, P., & Morrow, J. (1994). Assessing the developmental components of managerial jobs. Journal of Applied Psychology, 79(4), 544-560.

Mintzberg, H. (1973). The Nature of Managerial Work. New York: Harper & Row.

Mumford, M.D., Zaccaro, S.J., Harding, F.D., Jacobs, T.O., & Fleishman, E.A. (2000). Leadership skills for a changing world: Solving complex social problems. Leadership Quarterly, 11(1), 11-35.

Northouse (2016). Leadership: Theory and Practice (7th Ed). Thousand Oaks, CA: Sage Publications Inc.

Padilla, A. Hogan, R., & Kaiser, R.B. (2007). The toxic triangle: Destructive leaders, susceptible followers, and conducive environments. The Leadership Quarterly, 18, 180.

Parker, G.M. (1990). Team Players and Teamwork. San Francisco: Jossey-Bass.

Picardi, C.A. (2019). Recruitment and Selection: Strategies for Workforce Planning & Assessment. Thousand Oaks, CA: Sage Publications Inc.

Rotter, J.B. (1966). Generalized expectancies for internal versus external control of reinforcement. Psychological Monographs, 80(609).

Schein, E.H. (1992). Organizational Culture and Leadership (2nd Ed). San Francisco: Jossey-Bass.

Schumann, P.L. (2001). A moral principles framework for human resource management ethics. Human Resource Management Review, 11, 93-111.

Sternberg, R.J. (December 2003). WICS: A model of leadership in organizations. Academy of Management Learning and Education, 387.

Stogdill, R.M. (1948). Personal factors associated with leadership: A survey of the literature. Journal of Psychology, 25, 35-71.

Stogdill, R.M. (1974). Handbook of Leadership: A Survey of Theory and Research. New York, NY: Free Press.

The Peter F. Drucker Foundation (1996). The Leader of the Future. San Francisco: Jossey-Bass.

Yukl, G. (1987). A new taxonomy for integrating diverse perspectives on managerial behavior. Paper presented at the American Psychological Association meeting, New York.

Yukl, G. (1989). Managerial leadership: A review of theory and research. Journal of Management, 15, 251-289.

Yukl, G. (1998). Leadership in Organizations (4th Ed). Upper Saddle River, NJ: Prentice-Hall.

Zaccaro, S.J., Rittman, A.L., & Marks, M.A. (2001). Team leadership. Leadership Quarterly, 12, 451-483.

Made in United States
Troutdale, OR
05/22/2025